Waiting and Loving

Waiting and Loving

*Thoughts Occasioned by the Illness
and Death of a Parent*

Martha Whitmore Hickman

AN AUTHORS GUILD BACKINPRINT.COM EDITION

Waiting and Loving

Thoughts Occasioned by the Illness and Death of a Parent

All Rights Reserved © 1984, 2000 by Martha Whitmore Hickman

No part of this book may be reproduced or transmitted in any form or by any means, graphic, electronic, or mechanical, including photocopying, recording, taping, or by any information storage or retrieval system, without the permission in writing from the publisher.

AN AUTHORS GUILD BACKINPRINT.COM EDITION

Published by iUniverse.com, Inc.

For information address:

iUniverse.com, Inc.

620 North 48th Street, Suite 201

Lincoln, NE 68504-3467

www.iuniverse.com

Book design by Harriette Bateman

ISBN: 0-595-00449-0

Printed in the United States of America

*To Mother and Father—
and for us,
their children.*

*Let us now praise famous men,
   and our fathers in their generations....*
*These were men of mercy,
   whose righteous deeds have not been forgotten;
their prosperity will remain with their descendants,
   and their inheritance to their children's children.*

—ECCLESIASTICUS 44:1, 10–11

Contents

Introduction—9

Fall—11

The New Year—31

Spring—57

Summer—147

Epilogue—151

Thank Alfred University Summer Place for gracious hospitality at a critical time in the development of this manuscript.

Introduction

Why write a book about the death of a loved father? Everyone's father dies. What was extraordinary about this? There is no "ordinary" death. Yet perhaps when death comes in its most "ordinary," unsensational ways, we share that journey most closely. No barrier of shock or strangeness separates us from it, makes it seem an alien event. It could be *our* journey, *our* family. Among its cast of characters we vicariously take our place. Perhaps to walk through such an experience with others is to know our own life better and to be more at ease with death's later claims on us and on those we love.

But there is more. When my father died my son wrote to us, "I was sorry to hear of Grandpa's death, but I felt a sense of relief for someone who has done a very hard thing." It is a hard thing to die well. And it is hard to stand close, but not too close, and acknowledge a life that is ending and watch a loved one die. Its costs are high and renewed every morning, and so, in time, are its mercies. Perhaps here, too, we can learn from the experience of others.

So, to give company to those who must do a similar hard thing—and to honor a loved father—I unwind the pages of this story. And also with the feeling that it is not only a father's death, and a family's ability to love and to wait and to sustain that are at issue here, but that much of the meaning of life itself stands in these long shadows and comes out into the sun.

There is not much faith talk—though there is some—in this book. There wasn't in my father's life, either. An idiom from a high school French class comes to mind—*Cela va sans dire—It goes without saying.* In the most basic meaning of the Incarnation, where there is ultimate illness, it is acts of love—visiting, holding, affirming, listening, making arrangements—that are the bread of life. They are the Bread of Life. *Cela va sans dire.*

Fall

They're not coming....

Nov. 9. Mother and Father called, saying they won't be able to come for Thanksgiving. Father didn't know why; he just didn't feel strong enough to make the trip. Maybe if he stayed home and got some of his cases finished up (even at eighty, he is still practicing law), he could gather the extra strength, and they could come later. They were sorry. They knew we were disappointed. Maybe they could come in the spring.

Even as they told me, I sat down on the chair and wept. I have the feeling that I have been holding out for this—that if I could just get them here, I could be at ease about the house—because they have never seen it, and it has meant so much to me that they should come here and be in our home. We have lived in parsonages. We have never had a home of our own before. But now Hoyt's job has changed, and we have moved to the South. I have needed to have them here, as a kind of blessing. I want to take care of them in my house, as they took care of me through the years of my childhood in a home that is magic to me yet. But I am afraid now they will never come, and the sorrow of that overtakes me—he will never be strong enough to come, he will never see us here. The premonition that it is so stays in the back of my mind, and I weep as I am getting the supper or straightening up the living room—he will never see my house. She may come, for she is stronger, but he? I fear he will not come.

It is more than that, too. He keeps getting infections, taking weeks to recover. Some day...It is the shaking of the foundations. That which has stood between me and chaos, me and the world, me and death. My parents, intact. *Please. Let it be that way.*

Nov. 15. Thanksgiving is still more than a week away, and Mary has called. Mother had called her, wanted to tell one of the children, but didn't think she needed to call us all, because it didn't look like a serious illness. After supper, Father felt dizzy and had put his head down against the table. She got him to the sofa and called the doctor. He thought it seemed like an inner ear infection and Father should go to the hospital—he'll probably be there less than a week. They speculated it may have been caused by Father's holding his head in a sideways position much of the afternoon as he was gluing the broken leg of a chair.

Well, it's a good thing now that they didn't plan to come.

Nov. 17. I called home tonight. Mother had come back from the hospital. Father was feeling much better, but still very weak. They haven't allowed him out of bed, and there is no mention of when he will come home. I asked her how she was, and she said, "Oh, all right." She is seventy-nine herself and depends on him to do things for her. We are so far away—a thousand miles.

I hung up wondering, *When will he go home?*

Home for him is that white frame house they moved into the day I was two years old. Another five years and they will have lived there half a century. They built the house on what had been part of my grandfather's farm. When we were young, my sister and I picked daisies and devil's paintbrush and Queen Anne's lace from the fields on either side of us. Today the street is lined with houses.

My father's name is writ large on his house and on the

gardens that grow around it and at the edge of the half-acre lot—level in front, sloping down a hill to a level stretch in back. I see him in the house, sitting in his favorite blue and white wing chair in the living room, the newspaper tilting out before him, his head nodding forward occasionally in a nervous gesture of apparent chafing at the neck, even though his collar lies loose around his throat. I see him in his gardening clothes of worn khaki pants, old sneakers, and a sleeveless cotton undershirt, thinning the rhubarb, planting zinnias and chrysanthemums and baby's breath in the garden at the base of the hill, or working at the iris bed at the north border of the lot next to the patch of tall grass and milkweed and field flowers. "You need something wild around the place," he says. I see him planting pansies by the front door or tying up the rosebushes that each June trail cascades of red and pink over the trellises of the side porch. I see him, a much younger man, standing in front of the bathroom mirror, lathering his face with shaving cream and singing an old song from Amherst College:

> Oh, sometimes I live in the city,
> And sometimes I live in the town,
> And sometimes the wild notion comes into my head—

He pauses, and continues—very basso:

> To jump in the river, and drown.

I see him in the cellar, shaking down the ashes in the days before the furnace was converted to oil, or sliding the wire basket of the cornpopper back and forth over the furnace fire, while we children stand watching as the thin layer of yellow kernels explodes into white popcorn, straining against the lid.

It is fall now, and the gardens will wait for him, but when will he get home to see them again?

Nov. 23. Thanksgiving. We talked with Mother again. She had been down to see Father. He has been there for more than a week now, and the doctor doesn't say anything about his coming home. The dizziness has gone, but he has no strength. I had talked with Celia, next door. She knew how eagerly I had looked forward to my parents' coming. She groaned when I told her my father had an inner ear infection. She had one once and was in bed for two weeks, but it was easily a month before she felt well again. I told Mother. She will tell Father, so he won't be too discouraged with his progress.

If he doesn't seem better soon I'll fly up for a few days. I am drawn to them, drawn to being there. It is as though my heart is there already. Do I think that if I go I can make it all right? Am I being the "good child," going home? Of their four children I am most able to, now. Do I want them for myself at last? These are possible threads. Mostly it is that I love them and want to be with them in their frailty and need.

Nov. 28. I called. Father may be a little stronger, but he is still very weak. It sounds ominous, a cloud of darkness when I think of it. Mother goes to see him every day—one of the neighbors takes her, or she gets a cab. She hasn't driven for several years. "I feel stupid," she said. "The car just sits there in the driveway."

"I'll use it, when I come," I told her.

I'm going up next week to see her and visit with him in the hospital. My parents' need of me is greater than my children's right now, though I shall miss the leaven of their healthy chatter, the scattered agenda of their lives, the dailiness and diffusion of "ordinary time"—that charming designation in the church year. *God, give us enough "ordinary time" to put between our crises, give our nerves a rest.* Yet there is something energizing, simplifying, about crisis—a sense of I know (at last?) what I should be doing.

The hospital where I shall visit my father is familiar to me—my place, too, my holy ground. As a child of five I incurred a streptococcus bloodstream infection. It was before the days of antibiotics, and I was deathly ill. I had emergency surgery in that hospital, and my father visited me faithfully, at least twice a day. I received more of his undivided attention there than I got at home. The discovery of my father as a loving and present parent during my hospitalization and long months of convalescence was one of the legacies of a frightening and painful time. I have carried other things, too, from that year of illness and recovery—a knowledge of the closeness of death and of the fragility of life and a sense that its gifts are never to be taken for granted. A need to be close to others because we are all vulnerable and life does not give us infinite chances to love—only a few, only for a little while.

Father, stay a while longer and bless us with your presence.

Going to Holyoke....

Dec. 4. On the way to the airport I talked with Hoyt. "If Father dies, what will become of her?" I know that part of my anxiety is that they have cared for each other and if one dies the pattern is broken, the scale unbalanced. "Do you think we could invite her to live with us?"

"It's up to you," he said. "More of it would fall on you. But it would be fine with me. Think of your writing. Would you be able to do it?"

"I'll tell her," I said.

The flight to Massachusetts was smooth and uneventful. I got to the airport at noon, went home, then drove Mother down to the hospital. It is hard for her to walk. In the corridor I took her arm, she took her cane in her other hand, and we went along the hall, up in the elevator and, slowly, to the entrance of his room.

As we approached I saw first the outline of his body under the white hospital covers, then his shoulders and head came into view. He was lying on his back, looking out of the window.

"Father!" I said.

His head turned. A high involuntary sob came from his

throat. It startled Mother. "What is it, dear?" she asked, alarmed.

I went and put my arms around him.

"Marthy!" he said, the catch still in his voice. Then, "It is just that so much has happened." It is the emotional strain, I know.

He is terribly thin. But his color seems good, better than it did last summer, when we were all together at Lake George. I wonder how sick he thinks he is—he looked at me as though in his eyes he was acknowledging something I must understand. He was telling me something. Was he telling me that he knows he is grievously ill and he wants me to know—but we will not speak of it—we will not speak of it for Mother's sake? He has always tried to protect her. Once, when we children were little, he had to have some minor surgery, and he didn't tell her about it until the night before he was to go to the hospital. "Father has never wanted me to worry," she has said.

"How do you feel?" I asked him.

He was slow to answer. "I think I'm better," he said, hope in his voice. "I feel a little stronger than I did." I reminded him of my neighbor, Celia, and how long it took her to get over an inner ear infection. He hung on my words, so he can believe he, too, will get better. He plied me with questions about the family. I chattered on, about Peter at Allegheny, John at Oberlin, Steve and Mary in the new school, Hoyt's new work. I watched him as I talked. He is so thin, seemed to tire before my eyes. His speech slows. And in his eyes is an urgency I have not seen.

A nurse brought him something to drink. He drew the thick liquid up through the straw, his Adam's apple, too prominent, rising and falling. "He gets a dietary supplement," Mother said, and his eyes smiled at me over the straw and the nurse's hand. After he had finished he looked at the nurse. "Mrs. Baxter, this"—moving his glance toward me and there was pride in his voice and I heard it and was proud—"is my daughter, Martha. She has come all the way from Tennessee." His voice broke slightly. She nodded and smiled at me. "That's a long way," she said. She turned to him. "You feeling all right, Mr. Whitmore?" She straightened his bed covers and turned to go. "He's a pretty nice fellow," she said. He smiled at me, acknowledging the compliment. He told me Mrs. Baxter has a son who has just graduated from law school. It was her turn to feel proud. We talked a little more, and she went. "A nice person," he said, after she had left the room.

We heard the dinner carts and the clatter of metal trays. Time for Mother and me to leave. I'd be back this evening. At the door I turned to wave. In his eyes there was a hunger, and an unguarded love. I dropped Mother's arm and went back to kiss him again. "I'll be back tonight, dear." He nodded and smiled. There were tears in his eyes.

At dinner Mother and I talked about him. She wonders what I think. I feel weighted with grief, that he should be so weak—he hasn't been allowed out of bed since he went to the hospital. "The doctor talks about getting him started in physical therapy," she said. We ate slowly, close in anxiety and love.

Then I said, "Mother, if anything should happen to Father... If he doesn't get better... if you want to"—*slowly, slowly—it is very serious... the writing... it is more than that*—"We would be glad to have you come and live with us." I felt my soul shake. We have loved each other very much, she and I. But my long illness made us so close. I have had a hard time separating myself, standing free....

"What about Hoyt?" she asked.

"It's from him, too."

"That's very kind." She was strangely formal. I felt relieved and empty. "Of course we hope he'll get better and there'll be no need," I said.

In the evening I went back alone. Walking down the hospital corridors I thought how this is a world of its own, each room its own world, too—at its center the one who is ill, then the family and friends—timorous, hopeful, despairing, glad. I passed other visitors in the hall. We nodded. We are a family of many parts, many stories, characters in a play we did not choose.

Father was sleeping. The bone of his cheek stood high in the light. His arm coming from the hospital gown is thinner than a child's. Father! my heart cried out. He stirred on the pillow—"Marthy! How long have you been here?" "Just a minute or two." We talked about what he'd eaten for supper. "I did pretty well"—his inflection rose, assuring us both that he had done his duty by the food. He wanted to know what we had for supper and how I think Mother seems. "She is doing very well," I said. "I think so," he said.

I asked how he feels. "Pretty well. But, gosh, I should be feeling pretty well—I've been here three weeks." He mused. "Funny, it doesn't seem that long." He indicated the pile of legal envelopes by his bed. "I want to get at some of these office things, but I haven't been feeling very chipper. Maybe, before you go, we could look over some of them?"

"Sure, I'll be glad to."

We have all urged him to retire—though maybe his work has kept him going these past years when he's not been strong. He would like to taper off but has a lot of cases to finish. He keeps hoping he will feel stronger.

He spoke of his cough—he still has it. He has had a nagging cough for years. He had chest surgery six years ago, when a routine X ray disclosed a shadow the doctor thought was lung cancer. It was not cancer, but a benign growth on a gland that usually atrophies in childhood. He has gone for periodic checkups to the surgeon who did the operation. It has puzzled him—why does the doctor want him to keep coming back? And why does he continue to cough like this and to have his voice go hoarse periodically and then recover? On his last visit the surgeon, pressed by Father's questions, told him more: there were tentacles of the growth they could not remove; it was conceivable it would continue to grow slowly; at my father's age it was unlikely the growth would overtake him before some other accident of health would cause his demise. But, yes, remnants of it were there, and it could be causing the cough.

He repeated the doctor's diagnosis to me, and while he seemed at ease in his mind, he spoke of it in full detail. The relative nature of good news came to me again—what we will settle for when we have to. Yes, he has a growth; no, it should not kill him, first.

The loudspeaker announced that visiting hours were over. I stayed a few more minutes—it is a private room. But he was tired. I went and put my hand over his—I would cover him with my strength. "I'll see you tomorrow," I said, kissed him good night, and left.

I walked down the hospital corridor, a semipresence, watching the doors go by me—the rooms of the other patients, tired now, left with their thoughts. Then "Doctors' Lounge," "Admitting," "Record Room." I have left some part of myself there in the room with him, to guard him for the night.

Outside, the night was starry and clear, cold. The hospital stands along a road I used to walk on my way to and from high school. But my nighttime associations with this road are of walking home from the skating rink on cold nights, exhilarated, tired. Beyond the walk is a deep wooded glen known as The Dingle. It is only a short distance from here to my father's childhood home, and he has told me how, the spring that he was twelve and recovering from typhoid fever, he would walk down to The Dingle and watch the sap drip into buckets hung at the sides of maple trees. I see him—a thin child, sensitive and quiet—walking around, savoring the brown and gray barks of trees, looking up at the branches, still bare overhead but carrying within that bleak network all the promises of spring.

Father, sleep well in your bed in the hospital, across from these woods you have loved. May the darkness of high trees attend you and the feel of the bark beneath your fingers give you peace.

At home, Mother and I talked a few minutes and then went to bed—I to my room with the yellow roses on the wallpaper. I read for a while, then put out the light. Sleep did not come. The bed is under a window, and I looked out at the night sky and recalled how my sister and I used to gaze out this window, searching for a Christmas Eve Santa Claus to come trailing through the night. It seemed ages removed from me now. I saw the stars through the stark tree branches. Was one brighter than the rest? *Eternal God, Father of all mercies*...The stars are beautiful, brilliant, and very far away.

The night was heavy with portent at the illness of my father. I wept softly, trying to let it come to me—he is very sick, I must open myself to that reality, I must not turn away from it or try to gloss over it or to believe it is not so. He is very sick; he may not recover. I must accept the possibility that he will die. Yes, yes, I know. I felt comfortless and stricken in the darkness. Father, I love you. Do you know? Yes, he knows I love him. *Are you sure? Yes.* It is terribly important.

Unable to sleep, I recall how frail he looked when we first saw him last summer at our family reunion at Lake George. He came through the cabin doorway, moving his hands from table to chair to support himself, moving incredibly slowly, his face ashen, brows drawn together with the effort. *Father!* I thought. *What is it? What's wrong?* He hardly looked as though he would survive our two weeks together. But after a rest and some supper he seemed better, more like his old self. Our weeks together passed happily—he went for boatrides with us, drove up to town to the store, savored the gathering of his family. One of the grandchildren was learning to walk. Another, almost at the other end of the age spectrum of assembled grandchildren, had brought her boyfriend. Some of the grandchildren went off backpacking for a few days to a Maine mountain and returned to tell of narrow trails, high mountains, and beautiful wild scenery. "You'd have loved it, Mom," one of our boys said to me, mindful of my fear of high unprotected places. "In one place the trail dropped off hundreds of feet. On both sides." I shuddered. I was glad they were back, safe. All of us were caught up in the joys of being together, and Father seemed well enough.

One evening when we were assembled in the biggest living room he got to talking. He was always active in our conversations, though unlikely to claim the floor for an extended dissertation. But this time it was different. He began reviewing his life, assuring us that he had had a good life and that he really enjoyed living. He thought that when he had worked he had worked hard and that when times came for rest and recreation he had done that wholeheartedly, too. He recalled, with obvious relish and an atypical modesty, a conversation in which, though not present, he had figured and which had subsequently been relayed to him. It seems that two men who knew him were talking about him and the one whom he knew only slightly had said of him, "George is a nice guy, though I don't know how much fun he'd be at a party." And the other man had replied, "George *is* the party." He liked the story, and we all laughed in accord, because his humor *is* irresistible and pervasive and he does often seem, at first, like a quiet man.

He went on to say he had tried to be a good husband and father—he knew he wasn't perfect, but he had loved us all and he was truly satisfied with the course his life had taken. It seemed a kind of valedictory, and I wondered if that was part of his intention. I wondered when, if ever, we would all be together again. When he got up to kiss us good night—he was tired from his long speech—I could only whisper huskily, "Good night, Father," and turn away.

At the end of the two weeks, Hoyt and I drove my parents home. By the time we got to Holyoke, Father was feeling sick—had a fever and a queasy stomach. We got him to bed, called the doctor, got some medicine. By morning, when our family of six was to start for Tennessee, he was more comfortable, though still fevered and weak. We said good-by to him, and I went downstairs with Mother. I was crying, because he was sick again, not well at all. "He'll be all right," she said, reassuring me. "He's not going to die from it." I nodded, she kissed us all around, and we left.

She, standing there alone, waved to us from the front porch. In my mind's eye, I put him there beside her, his eyes moist with the tears of farewell, waving us off.

Their fiftieth wedding anniversary was this fall. We had talked about it at our reunion—would they like to have a party at home? We four children could come, but our spouses and all the grandchildren could not—some of us lived too far to drive and airfares were too expensive for large families. They decided that, during the course of the fall and early winter, they would visit each of us—first, Mary in Wisconsin for the September anniversary (she had not been able to come to the reunion and they were eager to see her), next, my family in Tennessee for Thanksgiving, and then Stephen in Oklahoma. At Christmas they would visit Esther in New Jersey, and that would complete the rounds.

Father did get better from his August bout, and they were able to go to Wisconsin. I had a postcard from Mother after they got back:

> We are home safe and tired. It was more of a trip than we thought. Dad drove the car to the airport so we had to drive it back. We had a wonderful quiet time, just what we wanted. Thank you all so much for the collage and the gold key. Next trip to see you. Much love from both to all, Mother.

We learned only later that he, as well as she, had requested wheelchair service for the plane change in the Chicago airport. He is proud and would have walked if he could manage it at all. It was a troubling omen.

Is this inner ear infection just an incident, in the midst of a graver illness? Has the chest growth caught up with him sooner than the doctor expected? Even as I asked these questions I realize how artfully I would, if I could, deny his frailty. Because I need them. Both of them. For each other, and for us.

The next day and the next I see him again. At times he seems strong and cheery, other times so easily tired. One morning we sorted through some of his papers, and he had me make priority lists of things to do—check on insurance payments, call Bill Hardy (his law partner), write to Boston *re* Reed estate, and so on, working our way through the pile of material. He has been a list-maker ever since I can remember. His favorite listing surface is the back of a long envelope, and I have seen a hundred of them covered with the hieroglyphic lines of his flattened and all but illegible handwriting, with crossings out and insertions, the corners of the envelopes crumpled from many trips in and out of his inside coat pocket. Once, in a fit of managerial enthusiasm, I gave him as a birthday gift a small leatherbound pad, very thin, with the suggestion that he use it for his lists—the binding would protect the pages from smears, abrasions, and crumplings. He thanked me for the pad and tried conscientiously to use it for a while, but it was not his milieu. One day several weeks later I saw him writing again on the back of a corner-frayed envelope, and I understood.

I am my father's daughter, a maker of lists. If I have a current list and have completed a task I neglected to put on the list, I will add it *ex post facto,* for the sheer pleasure of crossing it off. My third son, too, is a tribute to his heritage. A few years ago I began finding abandoned slips of paper with "things to do" crested across the top and, in handwriting almost as minuscule and illegible as my father's, his current list of tasks: arrange pictures, feed snakes, do homework, empty wastebaskets, and so on down the page. With my son's permission I sent a few of these to my father, so he would see how faithfully his lineage is extended. Now, in his infinitely slowly returning strength, it is what he wants to do first—make his lists of projects to be completed. I was happy to help him. But after a while he was too tired even to evaluate the papers on his bedside table. "I guess that's all for now," he said, closing his eyes for a moment. He never complains—only says, wistfully, that he wishes he would feel stronger, but he knows that takes time.

Back to Tennessee....

Dec. 8. I am going back home to Tennessee. I hate to leave them—he so weak, and she, accustomed to his help, managing so bravely by herself. I told him, as I left, that I thought he seemed stronger than when I came. It is the truth—he does seem stronger. As I went, I said, "If you don't get strong enough to come down to see us soon, I'll be back up to see you."

I heard a catch in his throat. "I don't know how soon, Marthy," he said slowly. He does not want me to expect what he feels will not happen—that he will soon be strong. We clung to each other—he is so thin, I could lift him with one arm—and I left his hospital room. In the morning, very early, I was on my way back home, to the house they have never seen.

In the plane I was aware of feeling such a backward tug of my parents' need of me. And then, how I looked forward to being with my husband and children again—to youth and good health and a whole different kind of agenda—my ambivalent escape.

I remember years ago running into a couple we knew in the Pittsburgh airport. They were going to visit his parents—his mother was dying, and they went every weekend to be with her and his father. I recall feeling what a terrifying mission this must be—weekend after weekend to be present to such sorrow. Now I understand they did it for themselves as well—that is where they would want to have been.

There was another side to it, though, and I am less proud of it, less willing to admit it—It is a relief to be away, to look forward to the sunshine and light of my husband's and children's health and love. It isn't necessary to weigh this completely now, know all its configurations. It seems important to acknowledge a kind of dual citizenship—we middle-aged children of frail and aging parents. Right now the juggling act is not difficult; it may become so. Right now all my compassion and empathy move toward them, even as I savor the health, the lessening of that constant intensity, the diversity of my life back home. We are stuck with a certain amount of guilt, aren't we—Why don't you love *them* with all your heart, and your husband and children with all your heart—and even yourself, with a little bit of your heart? "Love God and do as you please," Augustine is often paraphrased as saying. It's not that easy.

Someone to be with them....

Dec. 14. Esther called. She and Roy and the children are going to Holyoke for Christmas! She is reluctant to take the children away from home but thinks it will work out all right. Father is still in the hospital, though it's possible he may be home for Christmas. The doctor says he doesn't know—he'll see. If Father is still in the hospital, they can go down and visit him.

I've talked with Mother, too. She's going to get a tree, have a turkey—she'd not planned any of those things, with Father sick. I feel a great happiness—they won't be alone for Christmas. It's good of Esther and Roy. I'm sure the rest of our scattered family will be more able to enjoy the season, too.

Father has been getting up on most days. The doctor has allowed him to have a phone in his room now, so we can talk directly. It takes so long for him to reach the phone and speak into it—"Hello." His voice is slow. But he feels he is getting stronger.

Christmastime....

Dec. 25. Christmas. Hoyt's mother and dad are here, and all our children are home, and we are having a lovely day together. I called Father's number late this morning, hoping to learn he'd been discharged. The phone rang, and after a long time a click told me someone had picked it up, but it was many seconds later before I heard a voice—his voice—

slow, slow—"Hel-lo," the inflection rising slightly at the end, the sound extended in frailty.
"Father!" I said.
"Marthy!"
Then Hoyt spoke from the other phone, "Hi, Father."
"Hoyt!" he said, the pleasure in his voice compounded. "We-ell, how are you?"—the words came out slowly, as though he were drugged, though I don't think he is—it is weakness that slows his already deliberate speech. Esther and Roy had been down to see him already. Mother would come this afternoon. He had packages—he was going to wait until Mother was there before he opened them. How were we? he wanted to know. Had Hoyt's parents got there all right? And how were they? "Give them, and the children, my love," he said, each word leaving his tongue with an effort, thought of, articulated, let go. We had sent him a warm cream-colored shirt, patterned with a tracery of blue that matched his eyes. I thought he might enjoy it while convalescing, but now I wondered whether he would ever get to put it on. One of our sons had sent him a photograph he'd taken on our trip last summer—a picture of an old gnarled tree standing just below the timberline in the Rocky Mountains. The trunk is all grays and blues in the high mountain air. In the late afternoon light the earth looks a deep gray, the few leaves of the tree almost black. I knew the picture would speak to Father—the starkness, the history of the tree's standing against the high winds. It seemed just right for him now, but I wondered whether he would have the strength to understand the affirmation the picture was, of him. We talked for only a few minutes. He said, his voice rising, spacing out the words, that he thought he was improving a little. "Do you?" I asked, clutching at hope. "I think so," he said deliberately, trying to reassure us. I told him I will call the house later in the day. I sent him the love of all of us. We will talk again soon. I hung up and sat by the phone, my cheeks wet with tears. Hoyt came in from the other room and put his arms around me. "He doesn't

sound very good, does he?" I said. "No, he doesn't," he said, holding me.

After dinner, I called the house. Mother and Esther had been to see him this afternoon. Esther thought he seemed stronger than he had in the morning. He had helped open his Christmas gifts. He had joked with them about the weak broth that had come with his dinner. No, there had been no talk at all of his coming home, even for the day. They didn't think he would have felt up to it.

We wished each other a happy rest of the day and hung up. It was time for me to get some supper for my Christmas family here. Moving about the kitchen, slicing turkey, assembling bread, cranberry sauce, apples, and nuts, I felt at peace with the day. Father seemed better this afternoon. He is getting up each day now. The doctor plans to have him start physical therapy soon, to get some strength back. He has been weakened before and regained his strength.

How the season telescopes itself upon us! Christmas drops a plumb line down through the years! My father, a young man, sits at the end of the dining room table as we finish our Christmas morning breakfast, eating in desperation because we know we must—it is the family rule—before we go in together to our laden Christmas tree. My father leans forward. "I think I'd better go down to the office," he says. "You don't mind waiting an hour or two, do you?" It is part of the ritual, and we shriek our ritual protests.

It is later in the day, and Auntie Kate and Uncle Andy are coming for a noontime dinner. They arrive. Uncle Andy is carrying a laundry sack swung over his shoulder, and after an interminable dinner, during which we children are excused at intervals to go back to the living room to see our treasures again, we have another round of gift openings. Aunt Mame is there, too, an old lady in a teal blue silk dress, her shoulders hunched in age, her eyes small and bright behind heavy gold-rimmed glasses, her voice high and cracked. She is a widowed aunt of my father's half brother, and she lives alone in a dark house on Hitchcock

Street. It is my mother's warmth that draws her continually into our family circle. It is my mother who calls her daily to be sure she is all right. One day my mother will call her, and she will not answer. After several hours my mother will call my father at work, and he will go to her house and, going in with the key whose location he knows, will find her dead on the floor. She has had a stroke. My mother, consternation on her face, speculates that Aunt Mame may have lain conscious and helpless on the floor for hours before death came to her. The fantasy haunts me.

My father is to settle her estate, and one day my mother and I go over to the dark house to sort through some of her things. I have never been upstairs in her house. My mother raises the shades. The light is startling, out of character. We go over the contents of her bureau. My mother hands me piles of white underclothes to put in boxes. We carry the boxes out into the hall and put them by the bathroom door. The toilet in the bathroom has a varnished wooden seat and a long hanging pull chain beside it. I have never seen anything like it. We spend the whole day in Aunt Mame's house, sorting and packing.

I did not grieve over Aunt Mame, though I liked her well enough. My mother had told me I was her favorite child—"She was a funny-looking old lady, kind of scary for children, but you were never afraid of her and would go right up to her and talk with her. I think that was one reason she especially loved you." I suppose I felt some responsibility because of this, and my best friend and I would stop occasionally at her house on our way home from school. Going into the house, its windows darkened by drawn shades and the thick foliage of plants in wicker stands, and sitting on the edges of chairs and sofas, we would talk with her a while before we continued home. I think of her again, this Christmas afternoon.

I see, again, the first of the many Christmases Hoyt and I have spent with our own children. It is I who am in the hospital this time, after the birth of our first child and oldest son. I am so proud, so happy, and I know the smile does not leave my face. Hoyt comes, dons a hospital gown, and brings gifts for me to open. But the greatest gift lies there beside us, sleeping in his white crib. In his sleep, he moves, and his lip curls into a smile. My sister has sent him a gift. Its shape declares it to be a book and, clumsy and laughing, Hoyt and I open it together. It is A. A. Milne's collection of poetry, *When We Were Very Young*. Its recipient, smiling in his infant sleep, is two days old.

And another Christmas, not long ago. My mother had been suddenly taken ill, was hospitalized. After a few frightening days and some new medication, she began to get better and came home. See—it could happen to him, too.

Moving back and forth from kitchen to dining room now, getting ready for supper, I looked into the living room at my own family circle—my husband, our four handsome teenaged children—and, for these few days, Hoyt's mother and father adding their special presence to our family scene. I thought how blessed we are. There is love here, and laughter and warmth and good health, too. Warmed, made content by all of this, I felt at last encouraged to hope that health may return to my father, too, so far away. I realized I was singing softly to myself. "We gather together to ask the Lord's blessing," I sang. I smiled—a Thanksgiving song and it's Christmas. I know why. But—*Joy to the world*, I thought. *Joy to the world!*

The New Year

A new year. . . .

Jan. 1. It is New Year's Day of our first winter in the South. The grass outside is brown and green, and the air is almost warm. It is the height of winter. Earlier, we had one snow, about five inches of it glazing the streets and keeping the schools closed for a week. Some neighborhood children brought their sleds to the rise of the road in front of our house. They ran and flopped onto the sleds, and we saw them slide along the road for a few yards before the sleds slowed and stopped.

The grade of the road here is very slight. I think of a bright cold New Year's Day when I was quite small and my father took us to the hill at the end of our quiet street to go sled-riding. It was a rare occurrence for him to join in our play. I can still see him, standing at the top of the hill in his dark overcoat and soft felt hat—he didn't own a set of cold weather "sport clothes"—directing one or the other of us onto the sled and then climbing on himself, his legs buckling at the knees to fit the length of the sled. "All set? Let's go!" and he would shove off, digging his heels into the snow, and we would go shrieking down the hill, our spirits high in the bright cold afternoon and the rare delight of having our father with us.

I'm sure it is my father's illness that makes everything freighted with significance, that sends me back into memories of our life together—quickly, while he is still here. I reminded Mother and Father of that sled-riding occasion when I talked with them on the phone today. It was many years ago, of course, and neither of them remembered it, but were glad I did.

Father is going to physical therapy each day. An aide comes and gets him in a wheelchair. He has been practicing walking the length of a short ramp, holding on to two parallel bars. It seems a small accomplishment for a man who, a few weeks ago, was fully active, driving his car to work, doing errands for Mother because she wasn't strong. The therapy program was curtailed for the holiday, but the aide made special provisions for Father, so he won't lose the ground he's gained. "I know it will take a long time to get my strength back," he said, but he is encouraged nonetheless.

The doctor still has said nothing about Father's coming home. Mother thinks it's partly because the doctor knows how limited she would be in taking care of him. He's still not going to the bathroom unaided. "And I don't know how I could carry trays to him up the stairs." I suggested they could bring a bed down and put it in the dining room. We talked about the possibility of getting a practical nurse to help, when he comes home. I'm allowing myself to hope, on New Year's Day.

Tonight we had a festive dinner together. I gathered all our candles, of all shapes and sizes, and put some around the center of the dining room table, amassed some on the buffet. We lit them all—there must be fifteen or twenty—and lingered over dinner. Tomorrow our family will be dispersing. Peter will leave for Allegheny, and John will be off to Washington for his January term project a few days later. Mary and Steve will start back to school, and I will get to my writing again.

I hope to be able to finish my book this spring. If—if I am not too distracted by anxiety, I guess. I feel much of the time that I am living on two levels. On one level is my life here, caring for the family, enjoying them, working away at my book, participating in the church and community activities I care about, writing letters home. On another level, I am always there in Massachusetts, hovering over them, living with them, listening for their words and the anguish they do not express but which lie there at the back of their consciousness, too—staying with him in his weakness, and with her as she makes daily arrangements to take care of herself and to be with him, as they talk on the phone with each other but probably do not speak the words of the question behind it all—Will he get better, strong enough to come home, to pick up his life again and go on for a while longer? And if he does not, what then? What will the days and nights bring to him, and to her, watching and waiting, needing him, wanting him home? It is the substratum of my consciousness, and it is out of that that I carry on my life here and write my words on the sheets of paper I feed into my typewriter. It is out of that that my tears spring so readily in response to the loving questions of friends, "How is your father?" or when I am caught up in the words of a hymn at our small, close-gathered church—"When the darkness appears,/And the night draws near,/And the day is past and gone... Take my hand, Precious Lord,/Lead me on." It is a song far from the dignified worship tradition in which I grew up, yet how it speaks to me, reducing me to sobs. In my mind I hold my hand out to my father, because that is how, through the hand of someone who cares, love and grace are made known. By the end of the service, I have listened to Bill's sermon and the offerings of others, and I am composed again. Then we stand and join hands to sing together our farewell to one another, "Shalom, my friends... I'll see you again, I'll see you again, Shalom...," and I am again undone, by some subterranean touchstone of this music and the outreach of these hands on either side, holding mine. I can no longer sing the words or see, for the tears in my eyes, and, the service over, I try to regain my composure in a busyness of picking up my bulletin, putting down the hymnal, gathering my coat. I vow that someday I will come to church and not cry. "How is your father?" Bill asks me, seeing the anguish and the traces of tears on my face. "Actually, he seems to be doing better," I say, trying to manage a smile. He is not fooled. "It's a hard time," he says, and squeezes my hand.

Why do the support and love of friends move me to tears, when hostility just stiffens my resistance and provokes some articulate retort? What perverse barriers have we built around ourselves that we are so easily shattered by words of love and kindness? Is it that we know we don't *deserve* such a gift of love and trust and somehow in our Puritan self-derogation feel we have to be worthy of what we get? "Precious Lord, take my hand, / Lead me on, let me stand...."

Uncle Harold's visit....

Jan. 15. Uncle Harold is in Holyoke. He flew up from his home in Virginia, and he expects to be there for most of a week, visiting with Mother and Father and helping Father straighten out his accumulating and untended business affairs. He is Father's brother, his junior by seven years, and they have been much beloved of each other. I'm glad he's there.

Uncle Harold has been, in some ways, a mythic figure in our family. As a young man of twenty-four he was stricken with tuberculosis and spent the next ten years of his life in a sanitorium in the mountains of North Carolina. His cure was considered something of a miracle. He went on to have a distinguished career in the United States Patent Office and, with his wife (first, one and then, when she died, a second) and children, has lived in suburban Washington, D. C.

Because of his illness he was absent from my early childhood. I remember his coming to visit when I was about ten—a treasured visitor because, although I did not really understand it then, he had been so terribly sick and now was well again. I remember his sitting on the side porch with my father, having long talks on through the afternoon and evening.

To my sister and me he was dashing, attractive, a romantic projection of the heroes of our childhood, our first Lochinvar. He drove up in his black convertible, helped us climb into the rumble seat, and took us for rides in the wind and the racing noise. He was my final helper in learning to ride a bicycle. I had practiced at length with the bicycle secured upright on its standard; I had further practiced with my father holding one side of the handlebars as I wavered slowly and insecurely along the sidewalk; but, at my urging, he'd never let go to send me on my way. On one of his visits Uncle Harold offered to help and, running along beside me, holding the handlebars as my father had, he suddenly let go! The bicycle wavered, I felt a rush of panic in my stomach, but my feet continued to pedal—and I could ride!

He talked with my parents about a lot of things on those early visits, in long conversations of which we heard only snatches. He was learning to fly a plane, but he didn't want my grandmother to know. He talked about marrying—there was a woman he'd known since his early youth—they'd kept in touch with each other; she, too, had not married. He wasn't sure. He and Betty did marry at a quiet ceremony somewhere, and when they came back to Holyoke, my grandmother had a reception for them. We all went, and Betty was there in a dress of deep purple. We had a new aunt, and Uncle Harold had entered a new phase of his life.

In later years we often visited back and forth—either in Virginia or Massachusetts. Though he had episodes of tragedy and disappointment in the lives of his own children, Uncle Harold kept himself interested in, and available to, his brother's children, as though they, too, were partly his responsibility and his joy. Perhaps it was the missionary in him—he had rejected the Baptist faith of his parents, and while he was in some ways New England to the core, he had ventured into the more sophisticated social world of suburban Washington and found it good. He wanted to be sure we knew that kind of life was available, too. When my sister and I went to Washington for summer visits, he arranged dates for us with the sons of distinguished colleagues. He was the first person to offer us an afterdinner liqueur—an apricot cordial—which, as I remember, my sister accepted and I, half-bemused and half-shocked, did not. No one drank in my home. He became something of a name-dropper, but a very unblasé one, being rather continually surprised and delighted that he should be on a first name basis with some of the country's leading scientists and that he should be invited to join one of Washington's most prestigious clubs.

He and my father corresponded a number of times a year, at length and with care. My father sometimes showed us the letters he received. They began, "Dear Bo"—some kind of elision of "brother," I suppose—and my father's letters to him began the same way. Occasionally, when Father and Uncle Harold were engrossed in conversation, the special title would slip in—"Bo, do you think...?" "Bo, I was wondering...?"

And now he is in Holyoke to help and be with Father. "Harold has been working with Father's papers in the red room," Mother said, referring to the upstairs bedroom where of late years Father has kept assorted piles of documents, fragments of lists, annotated legal pads. I'm sure it eases Father's mind to have his papers in more comprehensible shape. He hopes to get back to them himself, but it has occurred to him, I know, as it has to Harold and to all of us—what if he can't?

Jan. 20. Uncle Harold has gone back to Virginia. He promises to return later. I asked Mother how he found Father to be. "About as he'd expected, I guess," she said. He thought Father was very thin. He said they'd had some good talks. What had they talked about, these two, with their more than seventy years of shared memory, and now to find themselves, and each other, men whom they would in their youth have considered old? "Bo, I was wondering...?"

Wondering what, Father? Can you talk with him about it, find some quietude for the thoughts that must hum around the possibility of the end of life, like a swarm of bees?

Going to Massachusetts again. . . .

Feb. 1. I plan to go to Massachusetts again soon. It's been two months since I was there. It's not only that they need me. I need them, while there is time. I remember, after Mother had been very sick two years ago, I stopped beginning my letters to them with "Dear Ones" and went back to "Dear Mother and Father." Write "Mother" while you can. Now, go and see them while you can. Yes, he does seem stronger. But why wait for some intensification of crisis to call you home?

Mary, from Wisconsin, and Stephen, from Oklahoma, have talked about going for a visit sometime soon. Perhaps we can stagger our visits to overlap a little, so we can see each other. Stephen will have to go when he can get off from teaching his classes, Mary when she can get time off from the library. My time is more flexible, though I would prefer Hoyt not be out of town when I'm gone, and now that he's traveling so much that may take some arranging. Perhaps I can stop and see Esther and her family on my way back here. It's wonderful to have a brother and sisters at a time like this. It must be much harder for only children.

Feb. 10. We have had sobering news. I talked with Mother today. The hospital has taken more X rays. The doctor reported to Father that one lung is perfectly clear, but the other is not—it showed some involvement related to the old growth. Mother had called the doctor for more information. There is evidently some kind of fluid in the lung, related to the surgery of six years ago. The doctor says it is that which is slowing Father's recovery.

"Does Father know?" I asked, after a long minute.

"I don't know," she said. "He knows there is something

there. Whether he thinks it is just the growth he had before, or more, I don't know."

"I think we should tell him what we know," I said.

"I don't know what to tell him—I'm not sure myself," she said.

"How are his spirits?"

"They seem good. He knows he's been awfully sick and that if he does recover it will take a long time, but I think he's hopeful."

"Does the doctor think he might get back home?" I could hardly ask the question, its implications are so loaded.

"I think so. He said Father may gain strength again and could conceivably come home, do some work, be all right for a while. We'll have to wait and see."

We talked a few more minutes and hung up. I sat with my head in my hands, wondering—*It isn't really new information, but what does it all mean?* I am glad, and frightened, that I shall be going home again soon.

Feb. 15. Getting ready to go, I have confirmed my resolve—to listen very carefully to his words and moods and silences. He may want to talk about the seriousness of his illness and feel he cannot with Mother—that it would be too frightening for her. Maybe he can, to me. I feel somehow very attuned to his nature. He said to me once last summer, "You and I think a lot alike." He'd been talking about a recent magazine article of mine and some turns of phrase that had particularly pleased him. We have shared some favorite things over the years. It was a pleasure to buy books for him because I felt I knew what he would like—*A Commonplace Book* of W. H. Auden, the works of Loren Eiseley, Frederick Buechner's *The Alphabet of Grace*. One of the last things I gave him was Sidney Jourard's *The Transparent Self*. It was, along with the *Amherst Quarterly,* the one piece of reading matter, apart from his legal and business papers, he kept on his hospital bedside stand. Jourard writes of the importance to physical as well as emotional health of giving one's self away, of revealing who one is, and I think my father, in some ways a reserved man who would have liked to be more free, hoped to find there some clues to a clearer kind of self-declaration and also, probably, the concomitant Jourard said would come—a greater physical health. I understood both the reticence and the hope. Maybe now, when my father may have something terrible and grave to say, I can listen for its coming and be with him.

Feb. 16. I got here this morning—took the bus from the airport, then Uncle Andy and Auntie Kate met me at the bus station and brought me to the house. The front door was unlocked, and I walked in. Mother was talking on the phone as I arrived. I heard her say, "Oh, here she is now!" and then she turned to me and said, "I'm talking to Father. Do you want to say hello?" I stepped out of my boots, wet with the snow of New England February, and, my coat still on, walked over to the phone. "Hi, Father," I said.

"Well, Marthy," the voice came back. "How are you, dear?"

"I'm fine. I just got here—good trip and all that. How are you?"

"Well, pretty good, I think. I think I feel a little stronger each day." His voice did sound strong. We exchanged a few more words, about the weather, the children, and Hoyt. He'd be having his lunch in a few minutes. Mother and I would have ours, and after we'd all had a chance to rest, she and I would be down. We hung up. I turned to Mother. "He sounds pretty good," I said. She nodded. "But Martha, he's so thin."

We went down to see him about midafternoon. Even after the phone call, I was fearful of how I might find him. He was awake this time, his head back against the pillows, the head of the bed slightly raised. "Well, look who's here!" he said, a great smile on his face. We both went over and kissed him, and I pulled up a chair for Mother and one for me. We laid our coats aside and sat down to talk.

We talked about how he feels, about my trip, about the noon meal, about the doctor's visit earlier in the day. "Did he say anything special?" Mother asked. "Nothing new," he said. "He poked around my stomach a little, asked how I was feeling. The usual things." As we talked, I watched him carefully. He is thin, yes, terribly thin. He doesn't seem worse than when I left him two and a half months ago, but he doesn't seem better, either. He's not under the emotional strain he was when I first arrived last time. I suppose he is quite used to his condition. If there is some unspoken burden on his mind, I do not sense it. He seems content now—as I am—for the three of us to be together. He thanked me, his voice husky, for all the letters and phone calls. And for coming. Esther was here, a couple of weekends ago. Stephen is coming later in the week. Mary will come, too, though she is not sure just when. It is gratifying to him, these visits from his children. I wonder, *Does it also worry him—an indication of how ill he is?* He knows that already.

He gestured toward a pile of cards and messages on his bedside table and, while he and Mother talked, I looked through the accumulated mail—his company of well-wishers.

There was a note from Cousin Martha in Sunderland. She is the widow of Father's cousin, Philip Whitmore—a much-admired man who served many years in the Massachusetts legislature and who had lived with his wife and family, now grown, in an old colonial house (once a tavern) on a high bank above the Connecticut River. My father's family had lived in that area for generations. In a college geology course I found "Whitmore's Ferry"—though the ferry had long since ceased to operate—on a contour map of the area, at a spot near Phil and Martha's house. Since we'd been children we'd visited them in Sunderland a couple of times a year—driving through the towns of Amherst and Hadley, past the onion fields and tobacco barns—to spend a Sunday afternoon sitting on the long side porch with the river off to our right and, to our left, a slim trail of waterfall rushing down the high bank against which the old house was built.

Farther up the road was Uncle Fred's house, long since sold to strangers. It was to Uncle Fred's house my father and his family came—much more slowly, by horse and buggy—when Father was a child growing up in Holyoke, twenty miles downriver. He loved to tell of the time he'd spent at Uncle Fred's during his convalescence from typhoid. He was to have gone for a week, but when the week was over he'd enjoyed the farm and his cousins so much he was secretly wishing he could stay longer. However, being a well-brought-up child, he said nothing to anyone. As departure time drew near, Uncle Fred asked if he would like to stay another week. Eagerly he said yes, he would, but he'd have to ask his father. To which—this was the part of the story that moved him most, I suppose because of the caring collusion on his behalf—Uncle Fred replied, "I've already asked him."

Uncle Fred was gone from the scene by the time I began to make visits to Sunderland. But there were other fine stories about him. It seems that the local train up through the Connecticut Valley would stop at Deerfield—the closest stop for Sunderland—only if the conductor was informed that "a large party" was to disembark. On one occasion Uncle Fred, who was quite a heavy man, requested a stop, and when the train stopped and he showed up alone, he responded to the conductor's remonstrance by saying, referring to his own considerable corpulence, "Well, I'm a large party, am I not?" He was also reputed to have addressed a political gathering, at which he was one of the two main speakers, with the words, "Ah, women. Ah, men," and sat down—the first speaker, to his mind, having talked long enough for both of them.

Uncle Fred was gone from Sunderland, but his son lived there in the house that had once been a colonial tavern. When Father took us on those Sunday drives to visit Phil and Martha, and sometimes to see the old cemetery where generations of Whitmores lay buried, it was in a peculiar way a going home for him—not only to the land of his forebears, but also to the bond he felt between himself and

Phil. They would walk out on the country road together, lost in conversation, and walking behind them, you could scarcely tell which was which, so alike were they in stature and mannerism and gesture. Always, when we waved good-by to the Sunderland Whitmores and drove off down the road, the presence of Cousin Phil would remain for hours in the tones and inflections of my father's voice.

On our way home from Sunderland we often went by Laurel Park, a compound of Victorian cottages among thick pine trees. It had been an old Methodist camp meeting ground, and my father's parents, though Baptist, had owned a cottage and spent a major part of many summers there. My father told us how, as an adolescent, he had helped operate the refreshment concession at Laurel Park, dispensing cones of hand-cranked ice cream and bags of buttered popcorn. In a confession of unusual guile he said he would sometimes dribble a bit of butter on the outside of the popcorn bags so customers would think the popcorn more generously buttered than it was.

Looking down through the pile of notes and cards, I saw other familiar names—the editor of the city newspaper, the owner of a local mill, lawyers my father has known through the decades of his practice. Other names, too—the girl who delivers the daily paper to my parents' home, the boy who, in recent years, has cut the grass and shoveled the snow, a woman who used to clean for my mother. Father was almost apologetic about the number of greetings. "I really am not too eager to have people know I've been sick," he said. "I don't want them to think I've stopped functioning as a lawyer."

Feb. 18. My days here fall into a pattern. It seems as natural as the busy life I left at home, and in a way it is strangely restful—life simplified to the terms of my father's illness—no frenetic adolescents or sudden community events, no agenda of a husband to make room for in mind or body. Each morning Mother and I have breakfast, then she calls Father at the hospital to see how his night has been. In midmorning I drive down to see him. He's in a private room so it's all right for me to be there, after the patients are bathed and the routines of the hospital underway. I spend an hour or so with Father and then go home. Mother and I have lunch together, then a rest. In midafternoon we both go to the hospital and stay perhaps an hour and a half. We don't talk all of that time. We read the afternoon paper; sometimes we just sit in silence together. I have brought my needlepoint to work on. Father may doze off intermittently. Nurses come in and out, bringing him pills, a drink of some nutrition-laden food supplement, the sherry the doctor has urged him to have before his dinner—maybe the drink will stimulate his appetite. Often nurses come in to visit a moment or two. They plump up his pillows and straighten his covers and ask how he is feeling. One nurse came to say she was assigned to work on another floor for a week and she would miss him. "So-o?" he said, pleased and gratified. She urged him to be good. "What choice?" he said, indicating his helpless condition. Another came on a Friday to tell him she'd be off for the weekend and back on Monday. She stroked his forehead gently for a moment and then, holding his hand, she looked at me and said, "He's one of our favorite patients. We all love him, you know." His eyes filled with tears, and he smiled at her, for the moment unable to speak. Then, "Thanks," he said, his voice hoarse.

When trays come for the evening meal, Mother and I go home and get our dinner. In the evenings I return to the hospital. Some days I've found him watching a news program on television. It's a good sign—for a long time he had no interest in such things.

I watch him, especially when I am there alone, for signs that he would like to talk about himself, his condition. He tells me of daily things that happen—whether he has been out of bed, what he did in therapy, what he has had to eat. But of any basic anxiety about himself—other than that it is taking a long time to get well—he does not say anything. I don't want to push him—it would be doing violence to his sense of his own privacy. But I am listening. Maybe I am afraid myself. Does he read that in me and therefore does not speak?

Talked with doctor. . . .

Feb. 19. This morning when I went down to the hospital the doctor was in Father's room. I waited in the corridor, and when he came out I called his name. He stopped. He knows who I am—we have met on numerous occasions before—he is a member of the church to which Mother and Father belong. I told him I would like to know anything more he could tell me about my father's condition. "Well, he has this chest condition, this lung involvement, you know," he said. "Yes," I said. I asked him if that was the same thing he'd had for the past several years. "Yes, it comes from the same thing," he said. "There's fluid in the lung."

"Is it malignant?" It is the question I am afraid to ask, but I need to know.

"Oh, yes, sure, it's CA." He shifted uneasily, accentuating my sense that he really did not want to talk with me, that he wanted to be on about his work. He looked toward the door of Father's room. "You have to be careful what you say, you know," he said. "He's very sharp. He understands everything." I nodded. My heart was a stone in my chest. My body felt constricted. "You don't think he ought to be told?" I said.

"Well, no. Sometimes if you say the word it scares them, and they just give up."

I nodded. He shifted his body again, as though he would be on his way. I understand his urgency, but I have my own, too. "Will he be able to gain strength, do you think?"

"We don't know. It depends. He seems to be doing pretty well now. We're going to do more tests. When we get the results of that, it may be that some chemotherapy might help him." He paused for a minute. "Well, I guess I better be going."

"Thank you," I said, and he hurried down the hall. I

stood there a moment, feeling cold and rigid, hearing his words—"Sure, it's CA... chemotherapy..."—then I went in to see Father. "Hi, Father, how are you?" I said brightly.

"Oh, I think I'm doing pretty well," he said, rubbing his hand slowly over his chest.

"Does your chest hurt?"

"No. My stomach has felt a little uneasy, that's all."

Outside in the car, I held my head in my hands. Cancer... chemotherapy. It is a familiar story. I have heard it over and over. About somebody else. I've heard that chemotherapy is only a delaying action, often not wise. An irrational choice. Reason has nothing to do with it. I want my father alive. Do we delude ourselves with a fantasy—that he will be able to come home, be happy, content, for a few more years? *Let him be better for a few years. One year then? Please... I am not ready.*

I told Mother what the doctor said. She's talked with him by phone. He's going to suggest the possibility of chemotherapy to Father. They'd have to move him to the Springfield Hospital for the treatments. He would have some nausea, but there are pills to control it. When the tests come in, we can all confer. I wonder whether I'll still be here. I'm going home in four days. Stephen will be here by then, and Mary.

Feb. 20. When I went to the hospital today a tall man with iron gray hair was sitting on the chair by the bedside, talking with Father. He seemed to be there on business. I waited a long time, and when he left, I went in.

"Marthy! Have you been waiting long?"

"A while. It's fine. I gathered that was about some business matter."

"That was Howard Joyce."

"Oh. I didn't recognize him." Howard Joyce is a man in his fifties, the son of one of Father's former law partners. I remember, growing up, hearing stories of how incorrigible he was, and now he's a distinguished lawyer with a law firm of his own. "He came to see me about some things," Father said fondly. "Howard is a nice boy." I smiled at this designation of the gray-haired man who had recently passed me in the hall.

We talked for a while, and then Father said the doctor had mentioned the possibility of his going to Springfield for further treatments. I wondered to myself whether the doctor had used any of the evil words—"cancer," "malignant," "CA."

"What do you think about it?" I asked.

"I don't know," he said. "I'm improving some. I've always been rather inclined to let nature take its course." I know he doesn't like to take a lot of medicine. He went on, "If I go down there and can't eat"—He slid his loose watchband up and down the flat stick of his wrist. "I'd just as soon not lose any more weight," he smiled wryly. "We'll see what the doctor thinks when the tests come in."

This afternoon Mother and I brought Father some raw oysters. We'd been downtown and stopped at the fish market to get oysters for our supper and got extra for him. How he enjoyed them—making a kind of ritual out of lifting each one out of the cardboard carton and holding it on the fish fork for a minute before he popped it into his mouth; he smiled a great wide smile and raised his eyebrows—a pantomime of delight—as each one went down. We shall have to bring him some more—there are so few things he really enjoys eating now.

Perhaps it is the thinness of his face—that his mouth seems wider than usual—that reminds me of how, many years ago, he used to astonish and entertain us by putting a whole cracker in his mouth at once. I don't know whether it was the departure from decorum that made it so much fun or the self-conscious delight with which his eyes lit up as he performed this bit of fatherly clowning. I thought of it today, watching his eyes light with pleasure at the oysters.

I recall another time when those expressions played across his face. I was recovering from my illness but was still in bed, and Mother had brought my supper up on a tray early, before the others had theirs. Father, who had just come home from work, came up to see me and stayed to visit while I ate. I had a large slab of cheese—always a favorite food—and I remember how he sat there, eyeing the cheese, licking his lips, making a great show of wishing he had it, saying, "If *I* had all that cheese and someone was sitting by me who *didn't* have any cheese..."—his face a pretense of disappointment. I remember the utter delight of this exchange—the shared knowledge that he wouldn't eat it if I offered it to him, the delicious power to keep it for myself in the face of the pretended request, and all of this resting on the knowledge that I had been terribly sick and now I was getting well.

Father, thank you for all the times you came bounding up the stairs to see me as soon as you got home from work. Thank you for the incredible richness of all that, and for your love, and for the way your eyes light up—for your children or oysters or cheese.

Feb. 21. This morning when I was at the hospital Mr. Appleton came to see Father. He's the minister of the Baptist church Mother and Father belong to, and he's not been there very long. He's an interim minister, retired, now called back to this pastorate until the church finds a replacement for the man who left several months ago to go to another church.

Mr. Appleton is a tall man with white hair and rosy cheeks, and there is about him an air of integrity and joyous humor, a sense that he knows some very good secret he would like to share. He's been to the hospital to see Father many times before, as have several of the city's other ministers, most of whom have known my parents for a long time.

My father has been a member of this church since his boyhood. He has served in various capacities, including deacon and Sunday school superintendent, and yet faith has always been for him a very questioning thing. He once participated in a Council of Churches Lenten Symposium and somewhat shocked the assembled congregation by saying, in effect, How do we know? How do we know there's a God, that the order of the universe cares about us in any personal way? I was married by then and away from home, but my husband and I were visiting at the time, and we attended the symposium. I was proud of Father's courage, though I was a little abashed. I remember my mother's face as she hurried toward us after the meeting—"What do you suppose happened to Father?" I remember my husband's reassuring her, "He was fine. The other people said all the expected stuff." But now I would like for him some "blessed assurance" in his extremity, and I wondered what this man whom I'd heard characterized as an "old-fashioned minister" would say.

Mr. Appleton stayed a long time. I don't remember many of the words that went back and forth between him and Father—a dance almost, so sensitive, responsive, were these two men to the reality of what the other was saying. They included me in the conversation and, from time to time, I said a few things, but mostly I listened. It was a conversation about love and trust, about whether we can hope that life has ultimate meaning for us, and so—the suggestion was there though the words were not spoken—that death has good meaning for us, too, and can be trusted. I know how Father is given to circumlocution—as a way, almost, of talking around that which cannot be articulated, or surrounding it with all its options, so that all the possibilities are there, though perhaps no choices are made. I do the same thing myself sometimes. It may be an unwillingness to take sides, to make a choice. It may also be—or so I would like to believe—an acknowledgment that though the options may be manifest, the answer as to which is correct may not be—no blinking lights, no voice from the edge of time proclaims it—and we are left with the mystery. All of this Mr. Appleton seemed to understand and to honor. But he was telling us his guess that the option that seemed right to him was that, yes, there is a meaning which is God, and the nature of God is love and can be trusted. What pleased me, seemed such an affirmation of Father, was the way Mr. Appleton absorbed the complexity and tentativeness with which Father spoke. Treating these with the utmost seriousness, which they deserved, he was able in a kind of overlapping way to tell us who *he* was, his own questions and beliefs, and that the hope which he had fit right in with what Father was saying in his more questioning and speculative way. It seemed to me a pastoral visit of the truest kind—an honoring of one another—and when at the close of the visit Mr. Appleton stood by the bed and prayed, I felt myself in a way unburdened, because Father had been able to express some of his deepest concerns to a man who truly heard what he was saying and, in a spirit of hope, affirmed it all and responded with his own self. Together they had offered it all up—an offering to life—yes, I hear you, yes.

I stayed only a little while after Mr. Appleton left. Father was tired from the visit. It was a good afternoon.

Stephen will be coming tonight. How I look forward to seeing him and having him here.

Stephen comes....

Feb. 22. I went down to the airport last night to meet Stephen. On our way back we talked about the new developments in Father's case—the admission of cancer, the possibility of radical treatment, and how Father is feeling. Steve feels that Father should know the truth. He is irritated— "Father's a bright man, an adult. He should know what his condition is." Part of the dilemma is that we don't know what Father does know. Does chemotherapy mean cancer to him? I don't know myself whether chemotherapy is ever used in cases where there is not cancer. I tell myself I'd want to know, too. But I'd want the truth to be good news.

After we arrived at the house and Stephen had greeted Mother—it was too late to visit Father tonight—he called home to talk with his wife, tell her he'd arrived, and give her the latest on Father's condition. She's an anatomist and understands the workings of the body more than most of us. They talked for quite a while, then we heard him say, "Oh!" as though she'd told him some good news. When he came from the phone he reported, "She said that kind of cancer is called a thymoma, and it doesn't metastasize." Oh! Then the queasiness in his stomach and the soreness in his wrist aren't new outbreaks of cancer at all. So maybe if the cancer in his chest can be arrested or even continue to grow but grow slowly, maybe it's not too much to hope he can gain strength, come home, resume his life again. After all, he's been apparently living with this for several years, and while he has certainly not been strong, he's been able to practice law, to travel, to work in the yard, to be home with Mother. I realize again how in a desperate situation we are content with small favors. Yes, he has cancer. But our hope is in the fact that it won't spread to other parts of his body and that it will grow slowly. Still, he is very frail. An hour sitting in a chair and he is fatigued, his face ashen. He needs the support of a nurse to get back to bed. Are we clutching at straws? Are we all denying what an outsider would know at once to be so? But we are not outsiders.

I went to the hospital with Stephen this morning. I am used to friendly greetings as I go down the hall, but this time I felt the wake of admiring glances. My brother is very tall and slim and erect, and with his dark brown eyes and brown hair and beard he looks handsome in his tweedy academic way. I'm proud for Father, to have so distinguished-looking a son.

I have tried to prepare Stephen for how thin and frail Father is. I waited by the door as he went in. He strode over to the bed. "Father!" He stooped to kiss him and then stood there, leaning over him, clasping his hand, and I felt the love pass between them like humming wires.

"Well, Steve," Father said. They turned to include me, and I saw they both had tears in their eyes.

I sat and listened while they talked. How had the trip been? How was the family? How were the teaching and research going? And, on Stephen's part, how was Father feeling? Did he hurt particularly anywhere? Did he feel he was getting stronger? What had the doctor told him since they had last talked on the phone? Was he—surrounded as he was by the legal papers and envelopes on the table—able to do any work? The conversation flowed, but the words mattered less than the feast of reunion. My brother had had in earlier years difficult vocational struggles; he had tried theology and literature before discovering in his late twenties that his calling was to science. Then he had to start all over again, working his way through catchup undergraduate work and graduate degrees and postdoctoral work and job searchings, to his present position on the faculty of a southwestern university. Now here Stephen was, arrived in all senses. My father was proud and profoundly happy with his son's happiness and with the love which, now, in the extremity of this illness, had brought Stephen home.

I stepped outside into the hall and fell into conversation with a nurse who had been caring for Father. She told me what a wonderful man he is, with his delightful sense of humor, his uncomplaining and appreciative manner, his eagerness to be the minimum of trouble. She told me her grandfather had been very sick and had died not long ago; she had been grateful for the compassionate care of the nurses who watched over him. She supposed that was one reason she enjoyed being with Father, because she had loved her grandfather very much. I thanked her and offered my sympathy for the loss of her grandfather. I acknowledged that, yes, Father is indeed a wonderful man, full of humor and courage and considerateness. But the question that stood at the back of my mind, which I did not ask her—this dear nurse with her grief and her love—was, *And do you, too, think my father, is dying? Tell me he isn't, if you can.*

Mary's coming. . . .

Feb. 23. This morning Stephen and I went to the hospital again. It's a very different place in the morning from either afternoon or evening. Nurses and doctors hurry about. The PA system calls out doctors' names, orderlies wheel patients through the halls.

Father's room seems to hold some special attraction—he has been there a long time now, and I'm sure the nurses are genuinely fond of him. Today there were not only the regular floor nurses who came in and out, to straighten him up and ask how he is feeling, but a whole covey of new nurses' aides came to visit, too.

In the room next to his a long-time friend and neighbor, Jack Adams, is recovering from cataract surgery. Today he came in to chat with Father and Steve and me, wearing his green plastic eye patch over one eye. After several of the nurses had been in on their solicitous visits to Father, Mr. Adams said, "George, you certainly attract the women in here. How come I don't have them in such droves coming to see me?" Father looked appraisingly at him and said, "It's the eye patch, Jack." We all laughed.

After he'd gone, a young aide named Sally came in with two friends she wanted to have meet Father. She was extolling his virtues to her friends, and suddenly she stopped and turned and said to him, "Are you married?" "Just once," he said, conspiratorially. It's wonderful his sense of humor stays with him.

Today Steve and I talked with Father about the prospects of chemotherapy. The tests' results are not in yet—they won't be by the time I leave. Our conversation was all speculative. Father thinks he's made progress. He thinks he's eating better. He's loathe to start on something of uncertain value. The doctors will confer.

In the hall on the way out, we saw our neighbor, Francine, who is on the hospital's nursing school faculty. She's been in and out to see Father often. We asked her what she thinks of chemotherapy in his case. "It won't cure things," she said, "but it might delay them." She's recently been to a seminar on the care of elderly and ill patients, and she talked about the cruelty of using radical experimental methods to prolong life in the terminally ill. Stephen and I were in complete accord—we didn't want that. "But on the other hand, chemotherapy might help," she said. "It might make him able to come home, lead a fairly normal life for a few years more." I shall be gone by the time the decision is made. In a way I'm glad to leave it to the rest of them. But how I yearn for him to get better!

I go home on the early plane tomorrow. Steve and I went to the hospital tonight. We didn't stay long, because we had to drive to the airport to pick up Mary, who is coming in for a few days' visit. Tonight's visit was heavy with sorrow and hope and farewell. I told Father I thought he seemed better than when I had come a week ago, although I knew it was slow and I hoped he didn't get too discouraged. I told him we would be calling and writing and holding them in our thoughts.

When it was time for me to go, we held on to each other, both of us crying, needing to say good-by and trying to cheer one another but realizing the outlook for him was uncertain at best. I hugged him again, my face against the gaunt wet boniness of his cheek, and then, looking into his eyes, I said good-by once more and started to leave the room. Steve was standing at the foot of the bed, tears running down his cheeks, too. "I'll see you tomorrow, Dad," he said. When we were at the door, Father called out again. "Marthy?" I turned back. He was propped against his pillows, and the light from his bed lamp shafted through his gray hair and held the bones of his thin face in high relief. "I think," he said, his voice hoarse from the effort and the emotion, "I think I'm going to get better." I looked back at him, feasting my eyes once more on the reality of his presence—gaunt and thin, frail and weak, at least he is *here*. "Thank you for trying," I said.

We left and walked down the hall. Was ever a man clinging so valiantly to life?

Mary's plane was on time. We saw her in the crowd, her light brown hair curling around her face, her eyes lighting up when she saw us. She was wearing a sheepskin coat, the color of her hair. I'm not used to seeing her in winter clothes—our visits are usually summer reunions. She and Steve will be here a few days together, then Steve will go and she'll stay on a little longer. On the way back from the airport we talked about Father's condition and what the future may hold. The three of us sat up very late, after Mother had gone to bed, and talked about Mother and Father and ourselves and each other and our anxiety about the future. If Father dies, what will Mother do? Would she be happiest staying on in this house—alone or with a companion if one can be found—in this city where she has lived for fifty years. Would she come to live with one of us? Which one? Even Esther, in New Jersey, lives far from here, where our mother's life has been.

I told them Hoyt and I have offered to have her come and live with us.

At first they were silent. Then Mary said, "That's very good of you. Are you sure? Mother is dear, but she wants a lot of waiting on." It's true, though she's been managing well, doing more for herself.

"No, I'm not. It's a bit scary." I paused. "She took care of her mother." I remember her stories of going to Troy, taking her babies with her—the shadowed reminder in her eyes as she has told of it—"I took care of *my* mother." "Besides," I said, "she took care of me when I was sick."

"That's just it," Stephen said. He hesitated. "Maybe with the four of us, Mother could spend three months a year with each family..." His voice drifted off.

More silence. I said, "What I really want is for Father to get better and come home and for them to live on in this house forever."

Feb. 24. Mary and Stephen got up very early—we had only a few hours of sleep—to take me to the airport. A light snow was falling, but the roads weren't slippery yet. I urged them to let me off and start back before the storm got worse. We hugged each other in the car, and I got out and

The New Year 55

went into the terminal, my suitcase in my hand. I checked in, then went to the waiting area. A party of about fifty people—they appeared to be Black Muslims, all wearing black—was waiting to board the plane, too. A leader was checking them off on a list. They must have had a special reduced fare rate because later, when the stewardess brought me my breakfast, she offered none to my seat mate and, looking around, I saw that none of the other members of the party seemed to be eating, either. Or did they have some dietary restriction?

I ate my omelet and coffee cake in embarrassed silence, wondering whether I should try, in some joking way, to mention my uneasiness to the man beside me. But I didn't know what to say. The whole thing had an air of unreality, like a Fellini movie. The group got off in Pittsburgh, and for the rest of the way I was almost alone in the plane.

By the time I arrived in Nashville I was tired from the trip and the strain of leaving. Hoyt met me at the airport, and we came home. As the hours have gone on and the children have come home from school and we are together, I have felt cherished and cared for, glad to be home, have felt some of the intensity of my anxiety for my father drain slowly into the earth of the whole person I am—that I am not only a grown daughter concerned for my sick and perhaps dying father and for my mother, who, faced with so great a loss, has desperate needs from me, too. But I take my place against a larger background—that I am also wife, mother, writer, friend, that the antennae of my life are out in many directions, and I am nurtured, supported, by all of these—even by the fields, sand, water, sky, the earth itself.

Springfield . . . chemotherapy. . . .

March 2. I talked with Mother. They're going to go ahead with the chemotherapy. Stephen and Mary have both gone back to their homes. Before they left they talked at length with Francine—the neighbor who's a nurse. They're all satisfied that going ahead with the treatment is the best course. I called Stephen after I'd talked with Mother. Yes, he thought it was a wise step to take, and so, he was sure, did Father. I was glad for the reassurance.

Mother is concerned about how she'll get to Springfield to see Father. The roundtrip cab fare is fifteen dollars. We've all told her we'd be glad to share the expense. By all means, for her own sake and Father's—and ours—she should go when she can. She thinks maybe Auntie Kate and Uncle Andy may offer to drive her, too.

Father will go down by ambulance in a few days. It'll be about two weeks after the treatments are completed before they'll know whether they've helped.

Spring

March 5. Spring is starting here—our first in Tennessee. It's a couple of months earlier than we're used to, in New England or Pennsylvania. It's still early March, and some days the air is warm as summer, a caress against the face. Trees and bushes we've not known burst in a pink and red profusion along the sides of a hundred streets we pass on our way around the city—as though they are nothing, as though they don't stab the heart to wakefulness, take the breath away. There's a tree beside our driveway. Since we came, last June, it has sat there, a perfectly ordinary green-leafed, gray-barked tree. Now it is transformed. There are no leaves on it yet, but suddenly, from out of the dark gray bark tiny sprays of deep pink blossoms have sprung. I'm told it's a redbud tree. In the morning I stand by it, close in among the branches, lightly touching the gray bark and the sprays of pink flowers, until the whole world sings in my head a crescendo of pink flowers and warm air and blue sky.

I remember last spring, when we were down here looking for a house for our impending move. We looked at one which an acquaintance of Hoyt's was putting up for sale. He was moving with his family back to California. They'd come from there a few years ago and, yes, they were glad to be going back. Then he said, "There are things we'll miss here, though," and he stopped and looked out the window—the redbud had passed but the dogwood was in bloom—and after a minute he said, slowly, "Spring in Tennessee..." and I wondered whether when spring came next year he would weep for this land—there was that kind of pain and hunger in his voice. Now, the redbud tree by my driveway calling me out again and again, I understand his longing, and I recall the line from Eliot, "April is the cruellest month"—though here in Tennessee it is only March. I remember reading somewhere that the reason spring pains us so deeply is that the world is bursting with new life, a beginning again, and we who watch it in hunger and amazement are not. It is that discrepancy that pains us, even as we rejoice at the world's loveliness.

I remember other pink flowers, paler, low among green leaves spreading out in a leaf cover in the woods, harder to find than this redbud that flaunts itself in the March-summer air. When I was young and living in Massachusetts, on some Sunday afternoon in May when the earth was just beginning to warm, our family would make its yearly expedition to gather mayflowers—arbutus is their botanic name. My father knew the place to go—he had grown up among these fields and woods. He knew the time—something in the air would bring him the message that this Sunday afternoon the mayflowers would be out. We'd collect some brown paper bags, climb into our car, and set forth, past the outskirts of the city, along a few miles of narrowing macadam roads, past the Brooksbanks' farmhouse, to a section of woods known as Rock Valley. We'd leave the macadam, turn onto a rutted dirt road, drive up the hill, take a few more turns to a place where a nearly obscured old roadway wound further into the woods, park our car, and get out. Each with a paper bag, we'd set out along the old roadway. After a few hundred yards we'd leave the overgrown road, climb up the gentle bank, stoop among bracken and moss, scoop away the crumbling dried leaves of winter, look for the glossy dark leaves, and then—the mayflowers themselves—tiny pink buds, growing along the viny stems, hard as twine. "I found some!" the first one to find any would call out, and my father's intuition would be validated— this was the time all right—and the search would be on. "Be careful not to pull up the roots," he cautioned as we moved among the trees and moss, bending low, fingers finding their way along the vines, clearing away the brown overlay of winter.

We'd stay in the woods perhaps an hour and a half, enjoying the moss and woods and the presence of each other, all the while dropping our clusters of flowers into the paper bags, moving from patch to patch, searching out new places where the tiny vines, flower-laden, bent their way. Then someone would grow tired, and we'd all realize that, yes, we were tired, too. We'd pick up our bags and put our noses into them, like horses to bags of feed, to breathe in the sweet acrid fragrance, and then we'd walk back along the paths and roadway, checking with my father as we came to forks in the road as to which way we had come—it was incredible that we had gone so far into the woods—the way back seemed much longer than the way in. Eventually someone would spot the car, and we'd drive home and fill our vases and low bowls with pink and green and bury our noses in them again to drink in that sweet woodsy smell of spring. For days the house would be filled with the fragrance of arbutus and the comradeship of the journey, our rendezvous with earth and spring—a gift not only of the earth and of the season, but of each other.

I think of it now that spring has come here too soon, and my father lies in a hospital in Massachusetts and cannot go to look for mayflowers—will he know, still, when the day comes?—and our hearts are heavy with grief at his illness.

I think of it all and wonder—*Shall I tell him about spring?* Shall I write to him that the redbud is out, the forsythia and daffodils have come and gone, and we have unexpected tulips growing around the base of a dogwood tree? Or will it make him more sad, because he cannot see it, too? The return of spring and the prospect of summer, the seasons for his working in the gardens he has loved, do not bring him much promise this year—may bring him, in fact, only a reminder that "April is the cruellest month," that while the earth is reborn, human beings are not, and that all those delights of ear and eye, of touch and taste and smell, in which he has taken such joy may soon fall away from him, as leaves from a tree.

March 7. I talked with Father on the phone this afternoon. Early afternoon seems to be when he is least tired, most able to talk. He sounded weak, his voice trailed along. He's going to Springfield tomorrow for the cobalt treatments.

He sounded calm about the whole thing, but he must be somewhat apprehensive—if only that the environment will be different. With his limited strength, how can he spare any in getting used to a new room, new hospital personnel, a new view from his window? I know of what small things security is built when one is sick—and to be *that* sick and have to be moved... After I hung up I called the florist and ordered a bouquet of yellow chrysanthemums sent to his Springfield hospital room. We haven't sent flowers before—somehow other things seemed more important. But this time a welcoming bouquet may help him feel at home.

I've noticed the last several times we've talked with him that instead of saying "good-by" at the end of our conversation, he says, "Good-by for now." My heart aches to hear it—he is feeling his life to be so fragile that he must reassure us, and himself, that he's not saying good-by for good, for death, but only for "now," whatever intensity of the moment, whatever grasping gratitude for presence and life, "now" means on this particular day. "Good-by for now, dear. Good-by for now."

March 8. Father was transferred to the Springfield Hospital today. I called home this evening. Mother was very tired. She'd gone down with him, ridden in the ambulance. Auntie Kate and Uncle Andy had followed in their car, to bring her home. She'd had to wait a couple of hours in the hospital waiting room, while the various admitting procedures had been gone through. His room is very pleasant—on the first floor, light and sunny, with a lovely view. Yes, the flowers were there, waiting. How had he seemed to take the trip? Well, he was very tired, but all right. She had called him from home this evening. The doctor who will direct his treatments had been in to see him, and he liked the doctor very much. They had talked quite a while, Father telling some things about his condition and history—though I'm sure his medical records followed him down there—and the doctor telling about the treatment he's planned. They won't begin it right away, though. They'll do some tests first and start on Monday. The doctor thought he'd be there about two weeks. And then what...? *Let him get stronger.* Father, I love you. Sleep well, in this place you do not know, with the pleasant room, and the strange and caring nurses, and the pot of yellow chrysanthemums on the table.

March 10. I called the Springfield Hospital today and talked with Father. He seemed in good spirits. He likes the doctor a lot. I asked when the treatments would start. "Don't know, for sure," he said. Mother had been down yesterday. He was feeling "pretty good, I guess." He seems content to let each day develop as it will—"letting the day roll over him," as Mary said one day as we were lying together on the grass out in the sun. But the day that rolls over him is compounded of weakness, and medication, and urinals, and trays of food in which he has little interest and, if he has any strength left for contemplation, for contemplating where he is now on the line between birth and death. We didn't talk long, but it was good to hear his voice. I can place him better in that hospital I have not seen, when I can hear his voice.

March 12. Mother called. The treatments have begun. The chemotherapy is in the form of pills, not injections. They're starting cobalt at the same time. No ill effects yet.

March 21. The treatments have been going on for more than a week now. Mother says Father doesn't seem uncomfortable, but all he wants to do is sleep. He'll talk for a while and then doze off. But his stomach doesn't seem to be upset.

I talked with Mother about where Father will go when he's through with the treatments in Springfield. He doesn't need acute nursing care, but he can't do anything for himself. One possibility is a nursing home in Holyoke—until he could go home. But nursing homes have no physical therapy facilities. Another is Soldiers' Home in Holyoke which has a hospital facility where Father, as a veteran of World War I, would be entitled to care. The Springfield doctor whom Father likes so much has sent patients there and been very pleased. It's usually hard to get in, but the social worker thinks in Father's case it would be no problem.

I asked Mother how Father felt about it. She said he is uncertain—he doesn't want to be a "charity case," a burden on the public funds. She said the adjutant of the Soldiers' Home had been in to see Father and told him there's no one in the city of Holyoke who deserves to use the facilities of the Home more than he does—which made him feel better. In a way he is fortunate to have the option. One wonders what other families do in this kind of duress?

It's too early to tell about the effects of the treatment. There is one very hopeful sign. There's no longer any trace of blood in the sputum he coughs up from time to time. He's had that for several years. The doctors have been aware of it and told him that since it only occurred from time to time, it was nothing to worry about. But at any rate it has stopped appearing at all—good reason for hope!

To Soldiers' Home....

March 22. Father is going to Soldiers' Home. We talked with Mother again today. It's only about a mile from where they live. "If I were stronger I could easily walk it," Mother says, but of course that is out of the question.

I remember when that hill on which the Home stands was all woods and fields. We used to walk there and see the city sprawling out below and, far away, the river and the South Hadley Falls bridge. I remember finding on that hillside the only patch of fringed gentians I've ever seen. I think it was on a Girl Scout hike that we came upon the cluster of several slim incredibly blue bells, upturned to the air. "They're fringed gentians!" someone said, and we knelt in the tall grass, the blueness of them, out there in the field where no one might see them, ever, in the course of their season, filling the air with blue.

Years later, as a college student learning of the romantic movement in literature with its symbolic search for "the blue flower," I saw those gentians on the hillside, and I knew that, yes, one would do well to look long for such a flower and assuage some hunger of the heart in finding it. And if, indeed, one ever did find it, it would be on a hillside such as this, the stems spiking down among the weeds and tall grasses, the blue flowers brimming the air with blue. Now the Soldiers' Home stands where the fringed gentians stood, and my father is sick and old, and loves flowers, and is going to that hospital—the next stage on a pilgrimage of which who knows what shape, and time, the end will take?

Mother asked the doctor how long he thinks Father will be there before, possibly, he could come home. The doctor does not say.

It's because Father is a war veteran that he is entitled to the facilities of the Soldiers' Home. Long before I had formulated any antipathies to war, I remember his donning his army uniform to go to the local junior high school for their Memorial Day observance. It seemed a kind of grand symbol then—my father, altruistic, brave, going to that most symbolically authoritative of all places, a school, to impart something of himself to the pupils and teachers assembled there. How tall he stood, how grand it all was, how mysterious and far away.

My father had been a corporal in the army. I knew only that the rank of corporal was an elevation of rank beyond the basic rank of private; to me he might as well have been a general. "My father was a corporal," I'd say proudly when my elementary school classmates and I rehearsed for our Memorial Day exercises. Standing in the brick courtyard of the school, we recited:

> In Flanders fields the poppies blow
> Between the crosses, row on row,
> That mark our place, and in the sky,
> The larks, still bravely singing, fly,
> Scarce heard amid the guns below.

I was addicted to it all—the bravery, the sad loneliness, the specter of men bonded in some mythic ethos...

> We are the dead; short days ago
> We lived, felt dawn, saw sunset glow....

I fainted once, during a recitation in one of these Memorial Day programs. It was hot, and we'd been standing a long time. I felt my mind go blurry, and I fell down. I quickly revived, but the scene became even more a part of *my* drama—the dimming words ringing in my mind, and the distant landscape of France, the Rhine River, the shattered bivouac to which my father had told us he returned one night to find his best friend dead in the cot beside his own. All of that formed a collage against which my father strode, his legs wrapped in khaki leggings, making his way back to America and to my mother and, eventually, to us, living among us as a citizen and father, except that once a year he put on his uniform again and went to the Joseph Metcalf Junior High School to represent bravery and romance and sweet tragedy.

He evidently left France precipitously. Or else he felt too carefree, with Armistice declared, to tend to mundane things such as collecting clothes he'd left with a laundress. I know that only because my sister told me that when she and her husband were going to France and planning to be in a city near where he'd been stationed, he described to her his eventful last days there, concluding with the request that she "Please pick up my laundry."

My father was in the Medical Corps, a fact which continually astonished my mother, who said he could hardly stand the sight of blood. When he went to give blood at the local blood bank, he always had to have extra orange juice, extra recuperating time, before he could feel steady to go on his way again—"And yet he was in the Medical Corps," she would say wonderingly.

He chose the Medical Corps because he didn't want to kill anyone, yet he wanted very much to serve his country. He tried twice to enlist before he finally made it—his eyesight wasn't good enough. On the third try the examining doctor, realizing the strength of my father's wish, left him in the room alone with the eye charts in full view, then came back to readminister the test. This time my father passed.

His experience in the army meant much to him. He had grown up in a strict New England Baptist home. His father owned a dry goods store, known for its integrity and lack of innovation. His mother was the daughter of a New Hampshire Baptist minister. She had come to Holyoke to teach school, and it was through one of her pupils—a rather sorrowful-looking daughter of the widowed Mr. Whitmore—that she met my grandfather. After she and my grandfather were married, her mother came to live with them (the Baptist preacher now being dead) and, according to my mother, dominated the household of her daughter and son-in-law, and the three children he had from his first marriage, and the three children he and my grandmother came to have, until her own death many years later. Thrift was a highly-prized virtue—no doubt a necessity. One imagines there was not much boisterousness in that family, that the style was probably one of reserve, both of love and of anger, that love was perhaps more presumed than expressed freely, and where "if you don't have something nice to say about someone, you don't say anything."

My father left all that to go to Amherst College—his first stage in breaking away. He entered Amherst with the highest entrance examination scores in the freshman class—a distinction my brother was to duplicate a generation later when he, too, entered Amherst. My father joined a fraternity. My brother's later rejection of the fraternity system was something my father understood and respected. But his had been a different time, the fraternity had been his community. He learned to play the guitar at Amherst, went to some fraternity parties, at one of which a young woman, upon seeing him, asked a fraternity brother who later spread the word, "Who is that boy with the beautiful eyes?" He was elected to Phi Beta Kappa, and he graduated with honor. John J. McCloy was one of his classmates, and when McCloy became high commissioner for Germany after World War II, my father took a special pride in his achievement and, I think, slept a bit easier at night because the affairs of Germany were in such good hands—was not John McCloy a graduate of Amherst College? He loved to go back to Amherst—to the many reunions which drew the men back in droves to "the fairest college of them all," to plays at the Kirby Theatre, to drive around the campus and savor its beauty and tradition, and later, after the Second World War, to stand at the top of the hill and look out over the new white marble war memorial Amherst had built to the memory of her many sons who had died in war. He took us there once, when he was old and my husband and I were middle-aged and our children were teenagers and repelled by all the symbols of war, to see the Amherst War Memorial. It was a beautiful spot on a hilltop, the marble monument set in the midst of landscaped terracing, with the names of the war dead carved into its face. It was a holy place to him, and he was not content until all of us had got out of the car and gone over and walked around it and exposed ourselves to whatever spell it might hold for us. It held none. It was an embarrassing time, because to him it *was* holy—this combination of Amherst College and his memory of his days in the war—but to us' and to our children it was a symbol of the hoax the government was then perpetrating to justify a different war, for which we had only aversion, and we couldn't share his mood. I, trying to make some affirmation of the moment for him, commented on the natural beauty of the place, and we all went back to the car and drove away, trying to leave our unresolved feelings among the landscaping and the white marble and the green grass of the hillside.

It was not long after Father's graduation from Amherst that he enlisted in the army, which then became the second stage in his breaking away from the confines of his family's style—an emancipation so complete that for three months he didn't even write home, until his mother made contact through the Red Cross with his superiors, who ordered him to write a letter to his family back in the United States.

When he spoke of his days in the army, he spoke fondly, nostalgically, remembering the French countryside and rides down the Rhine River with its legendary castles. He always spoke of going overseas as "going across the water," and I see him half-afraid, crowded onto some troop ship, joining in the camaraderie of men who came from different lives than his own but with whom he was able to be friends, brothers, even. I see him tending the sick and wounded, his gentleness falling on them like a balm, his tenderness making him wince inside—but he would never let them know—going on about his dreadful and healing work.

And now he, his body weakened and in danger, is going to the Soldiers' Home, and others will lift and carry and care for him.

March 24. The transfer to the Soldiers' Home has been completed. Father was taken from Springfield by ambulance. Mother says he seemed to tolerate the trip well. He's in a room with another man who is pleasant "but doesn't say a whole lot." The room is light and attractive, the nurses are friendly and kind. The hospital has its staff of doctors. Father hasn't seen a doctor yet—he probably will tomorrow. His own doctor will confer from time to time and be in touch with Mother.

Now the long wait begins, to see whether the treatments have helped. The hospital doesn't have phones in the patients' rooms, so we'll have to get our news through Mother. From the sound of things he's almost too weak to talk on the phone anyway, at least for a while.

Peter's home. . . .

March 27. The days go on. Mother writes, but not often. She says, "I haven't the heart." I write, and she and I talk on the phone. She doesn't see any real change in him yet. They know any progress will be slow. She said today that Father had spoken of an acquaintance who had cobalt treatments six years ago—"And now he can drive to Florida," he said, to encourage himself and her.

Life here is busy and full. Some days I don't think of Mother and Father in terms of crisis, but in terms of waiting. This week, though, Peter is home from college for a few days, and I must catch him up on it all, for my own sake, and because he loves them, too. We've kept the two college boys informed about their grandfather, but I wanted to tell him more—about the uncertainties of the treatments, about the big question of whether Father will be able to go home. As I finished telling him, I started to cry, and so did he. It is not the uncertainty of whether the cobalt will help that is the cause for our anguish. It is aging and death and loss in all their forms and knowing that my father will fall victim one day and so, in time, shall I, and so shall Peter, and all sounds will fail, and the scent of flowers will fade, and the touch of love will grow cold. We clung to each other for a moment—for a time we can be close, and blood flows through the body, and eyes see, though dimly, through tears, and ears hear, and the touch of my son is life to me. I went on about my work, thinking for a time that I can bear it—I have no choice—if my father dies. The choice I do have—which all of us have—is to be present to what is happening, and then try to reach out for love and support to others.

Waiting....

April 14. Mother still doesn't see any real change, and it's been several weeks since the treatments were completed. I ask her how he is eating. He doesn't have much appetite. He may be gaining a little strength—she isn't sure. His spirits are pretty good.

She's thinking of buying him a small radio to put by his bedside. There are no TVs in rooms, though there's a TV lounge down the hall. I'm not sure how much he'd use even a radio. I didn't say anything to discourage her. There's so little she can do for him, other than be there, which is, of course, the most important thing of all. She says the taxi company dispatcher knows her well and so do many of the drivers. I told her again today how splendidly I thought she was managing. She quoted her father's words from a long time ago—"Don't worry about Ruth. You can always count on Ruth in an emergency." But this emergency has gone on for months. On she goes, day after day, dealing with the necessities of her life—ordering her groceries from the small market that will deliver them, preparing her meals, getting herself dressed and up there to see him, dealing with her loneliness and her sorrow, wondering what to expect. Walking is hard for her, too, ever since the injury to her foot several years ago. Even when I've been home with her, to take her arm, it's taken a long time for her to traverse the hospital corridors. She said that if anyone goes with her now—Auntie Kate and Uncle Andy often do—she borrows a hospital wheelchair and has them push her along the corridors to the elevator and then to Father's room.

Uncle Harold back....

April 17. Uncle Harold has been in Holyoke again, visiting with Father. Mother said they did some business things, but they spent most of their time just visiting. Uncle Harold thinks Father looks very bad, is not at all encouraged, or encouraging—though he says Father may still be debilitated by the effects of the cobalt and chemotherapy.

And Esther and Roy....

April 22. Esther and Roy and the children have been to Holyoke again for the weekend—their first visit since Father was transferred to the Soldiers' Home. I called Esther last night, after I was sure they'd be back, to ask how they found things. She and Roy had not found him in such poor shape as they'd expected, given Uncle Harold's report.

One afternoon while they were there they took the children down to the hospital, and Father was brought to the sunroom in a wheelchair and was able to be with them all for a little while. Elizabeth is two, and Craig is four—they are the youngest of his fifteen grandchildren. Esther said they were dear, and Father was obviously delighted to be with them, though he seemed to get very tired, even with a short visit.

In some ways he's been able to relax and enjoy his grandchildren more than he could his children. Mary tells how one terribly cold day, when Mother and Father were visiting them in Wisconsin, Barbie, who was about five, announced she wanted to go for a walk with Grampa, and they'd each bundled themselves up and gone out in the bitter cold. I remember a weekend when we were visiting in Holyoke and Peter was just learning to walk. The New York apartment we lived in had no stairs, and Peter, fascinated by the stairs in his grandparents' house, wanted continually to go up them but was unable to get himself back down. For quite a while all of us catered to him, making the trips to retrieve him from the top of the stairs.

After a while Hoyt and I tired of it and would have put a stop to it, but Father protested, "But he *wants* to go up," as though that were the only thing involved. We all stayed with it until Peter grew tired. I remember thinking that Father would never have been so indulgent with his own children. As the grandchildren have grown, he's kept himself apprised of the special interests and personality of each one, delighting in their progress and exploits, though often he didn't see them for a year at a time. So I'm glad that, today, he was able to be with the littlest ones again.

A bad sign....

April 25. Mother said over the phone today that they've transferred Father to a private room, closer to the nurses' station. They gave no particular reason—there was no friction with the other man in the room. She fears it is an ominous sign. I asked her if he is getting up at all. I know the hospital is supposed to have an excellent therapy program. She didn't think Father had made any use of it at all.

April 30. The doctor has tapped Father's lung, taken fluid from it. I don't know whether that's for diagnosis, or because the process itself is helpful. I think the latter. Mother says he seems terribly weak. It doesn't sound good at all. When I talk with Mother, Hoyt usually gets on the other phone. Sometimes, when we're finished, he'll come to me and hold me for a few minutes, just hold me. It is immeasurably helpful, as though I can rest my anguish in him, draw from him some strength, just the sheer physical and emotional energy, to go on about the business of the day. It is one of the terrible things for Mother, that she has no one there, no body of a loving person, to help her deal with the pain through the simple reality of touching and holding. We can help her some, when we're there, but that isn't much of the time, considering everything. It's been Father she's drawn that strength from, and now she sees him failing. What is she to do? Who can hold her—to life, to courage, to comfort and love?

Mother said Howard Joyce has been in to see Father a few times. He is helping with the most urgent law cases. I'm relieved to have him involved—though I wish Father had consulted him sooner. We may need him in the days ahead.

Mother's called....

May 1. Mother has called, with a terrible message. I suppose in a way we have known it, but have hoped it was not so, have held ourselves from believing it, or that it was this urgent. Hoyt was not here, so I've been trying to deal with the message myself, with whatever help the children can give me. Today, Mother said, when she went to the hospital to see Father, there was a note for her that the superintendent would like to see her in his office. She went back to his office, and he told her—she said he was very kind—that he wanted to be sure she knew the gravity of Father's condition—that he is critically ill.

"Oh...," I said, and she went on. For this reason, the superintendent wanted her to know she may come to the hospital any time—she doesn't need to wait for visiting hours. Her voice was strong as she told me these things, and in a way I think she wasn't really surprised. Neither, I suppose, was I. But, oh, the sense of impending loss behind her words.

The superintendent had gone on to ask whether there are children in the family. She told him yes, there are four, all of us in different parts of the country. He thought we should be told how critical—the word again—Father's condition is. He didn't know how long it would be—"It could be days, it could be weeks." She thanked him, in a kind of daze I suppose, polite and gracious, a kind of digging of the heels into the moment, to keep from slipping, going over the edge of some abyss. Then she'd left his office and gone down the corridor, up in the elevator, through the halls to see Father—I see her, cane in hand, shuffling her way on that journey of despair.

I asked her, my heart pounding, how Father had seemed. She said he'd not seemed particularly lower than he'd been in recent days or weeks. He'd spoken to her brightly enough. They'd chatted about things at the house and about the latest cards and letters from the family. She asked how he felt and he said, "Pretty good." She asked whether the doctor had been in—the doctor doesn't make daily calls, just three times a week unless there's an emergency. The doctor had been in yesterday, Father said, and listened to his chest, felt his pulse, that sort of thing—nothing special. They talked on. She said nothing about her visit to the superintendent, and after a while she called a taxi and went home. She'd called Dr. Calhoun, told him what the superintendent had said, and asked if he couldn't go and see Father himself and give her an evaluation of how he found Father to be. He'll go tomorrow. He can't go as a doctor, he said—that wouldn't be ethical—but he'll go as a friend and tell her how Father's general condition seems. He'll call her tomorrow.

She wondered if I could come home. She didn't want to be alone. She needed somebody to be with her, to stay with her until the end.

My mind jumped ahead. My impulse is to go, tonight if I could, though it is very late and no plane could take me there until morning. But there is something else—it is a terrible dilemma. In a few days Hoyt and I are scheduled to fly to Chicago for a last gathering with dear friends with whom we've worked intimately for several years. It is a farewell time for us. We'll surely keep in touch with some or all of these friends, but we'll never all be together again.

I told Mother about it and that of course she wouldn't want to be alone, but depending on what Dr. Calhoun finds, I'd like to go to Chicago first, then come to Holyoke from there. Had she called any of the other children? Maybe one of them could come immediately. No, she had called me first. She was hurt and angry that I should even consider waiting. Hoyt is out of town until tomorrow. I would have to wait to come until then in any event. I'll call her back. We agreed we'd talk tomorrow. We each hung up, and I went into the living room. The children were there—Steve and Mary—doing homework. I told my story, and they shared my sorrow. When I described how my mother would like me to come right away and, unless Dr. Calhoun advises otherwise, I would like to wait the few days so I could have this last visit with my friends, they affirmed my need to do that, too. "Maybe Aunt Mary could go," Mary said. "Then you could go when your meeting is over." I nodded. What a help they are to me, my children. Hoyt will be home tomorrow.

It is heavy on my heart. I see my mother's eyes—accusing, hurt. *How can you? And what if he dies and you haven't come?* They are valid questions. They are not the only question.

May 2. When Hoyt came home, I told him of Mother's call. He is saddened. He's been in the family the longest of any of the sons-and-daughters-in-law. The loss is personal to him, too. I told him of Mother's wish that I come right away but that I have waited to talk with him and for her to hear from Dr. Calhoun.

We called Mother after dinner. Yes, Dr. Calhoun had been to see Father and had called her to report. He thought Father not as sick as the superintendent had led Mother to believe—he was alert, did not feel badly, talked readily. Dr. Calhoun didn't suggest any change in the prognosis—yes, Father is gravely ill, but he didn't see anything happening in a matter of days.

I was relieved, of course, and so was Hoyt, who was on the other phone. Mother still wished I would come immediately. Had she called any of the others? No, she was waiting to hear from me.

I told her, as Hoyt and I had agreed, that I would come after Chicago. Should things take a turn for the worse, she could reach me there and I could come immediately. She was angry and confused. Well, she would call one of the other children. I hung up feeling terrible. Hoyt assured me—there is no reason I alone should bear the responsibility of going right away. Of course she wants someone with her, but she hasn't even told the others of her need or of the apparent worsening of Father's condition. If it is unfair pressure—she must be forgiven everything. But I have my own needs, too.

Within a half hour Mary called from Wisconsin. Mother had called her. She will fly to Holyoke tomorrow—she can get away easily and is glad to go. She will stay a week and will be there when I come. She told me not to worry.

When I hung up, it was with tears of relief and gratitude. Mary is going. They will have someone to be with them. I will go to Chicago and then to Holyoke.

Back to Holyoke....

May 6. I arrived in Holyoke this evening. Last night was our farewell with our friends. We worked late into the evening. They had asked Hoyt to lead us in a final communion service. It was about midnight when we cleared the work table of books and papers and Hoyt set out the loaf of bread and the chalice and we all gathered round and he began to go through the ancient ritual of remembrance and covenant and hope. Our farewell remarks, after our four years with them, were to be the homily of the evening. When it was my turn I could hardly speak, but looking around I saw that some of the others were crying, too. I said they knew that my life was in turmoil now, that when I left Chicago tomorrow I would go to be with my mother and with my father, who is dying, and that was a very great sorrow. I knew that I might not see some of them for a very long time, and that, too, was a sorrow, but I wanted to thank them, each one, for what they had been to me over the past years. I had been reading a book on celebrating what is temporary, I said, and it had helped me in thinking of them and of all things that pass, and I wanted to remind myself and them that what they had been to me was a part of my life forever, and I was grateful for that. I don't remember the rest of it, only that it was a time of intensity and closeness and love. Later on when we stood to embrace one another it was with tears of love and rejoicing, because what we were celebrating was not only a ritual of farewell but the reality of love and that where love is—there are holiness and light and comfort. And going to bed about two in the morning and thinking of coming to Holyoke today, I thought, *Yes, perhaps I shall be ready.*

Hoyt and Bev and Jim came with me to the airport— Hoyt to return home to Tennessee and Jim and Bev to go back to their home in Denver. Jim, as a doctor, could help me interpret some of the information about thymomas and malignancy and fluid in the lung, but more than that as we walked around the airport together, I felt sustained by all of them—by Hoyt, of course, as I have through all the years of our marriage, and by Jim and Bev, too. I had the feeling that somehow, should I need them later on, they would be there. The time came for my plane to leave, and I kissed them all good-by, got on the plane, and flew to Springfield.

One of the neighbors had driven down to meet me. Mary was there with him—both of them waiting when I got off the plane. Driving up the dark highway, sitting in the backseat with Mary, I asked her how Father is, and she said, "It depends. Sometimes he seems very alert, full of his sparkle, almost his old self, and other times he is very weak—hardly seems to know we're there." The lights from cars streaked past us. "You have lost weight," she said, looking into my face. "Have you been trying to, or is it because things have been hard?"

"Because things have been hard," I said, and she nodded.

I asked how Mother was doing, and she said, "Pretty well."

"And you?" I said.

"I'm OK."

"How long are you staying?"

"I'm leaving Tuesday, unless..." Her voice trailed off. I understand.

We were home, and Ed stopped the car and reached for my suitcase. Mother had seen us coming and was at the door. "Hi, sweetheart," I said and hugged her. Her body is thin in my arms. "I'm glad you're here," she said. There were strain and sorrow in her face, but she did not cry.

I, too, am glad to be here. Tomorrow I shall go to the hospital to see Father.

May 7. In the morning Mary and I got ready to go up to the hospital. Mother would wait and go this afternoon. I'd never been to the Soldiers' Home before, though we have gone by the wide access drive many times. Its location is lovely. As we approach, the building stands a massive brick structure against the sky, at the top of this hill where once I found fringed gentians in the grass. This time we turned in at the driveway. It was like crossing into a new land.

We parked the car and got out. The air was warm, and a light breeze blew across the parking lot as we started toward the building.

"His room is on the second floor," Mary said. We went up the ramp and in the main entrance, into a large lobby.

A lone receptionist sat at a desk. An elderly man in pajamas and robe sat alone in a wheelchair by a window and looked out over the valley. After the bustling hospital where I'd visited Father before, this one seemed too quiet, nearly empty, the spaces too large.

"This way," Mary said, and we turned past the receptionist, who nodded, acknowledging Mary as a familiar presence here. We went through a hallway past the glass wall of an empty auditorium. "I think they have shows here sometimes for the patients," Mary said. We reached the elevator and went up to the second floor.

We got out into another hallway, off which is a large solarium. In the solarium two patients sat in wheelchairs far apart from one another, looking out through the glass wall.

"This way—the hospital part is through here," Mary

said, and we went through a pair of firedoors and came out opposite a nurses' station. The nurse behind the long blue desk looked up.

"Good morning," Mary said. "This is my sister, Mrs. Hickman. We've come to see Mr. Whitmore." The nurse smiled and nodded, and Mary led me to the first door on the left. "This is his room."

The door was open, and I looked in. The head of the bed was against the near wall, and the bed jutted out into the center of the room, so he lay between us and the window, his body barely raising the surface of the sheet. He appeared to be asleep. His head was in profile. He had a day or two's dark shadow of beard on his cheek. His Adam's apple protruded, a sharp knob, in his throat. His face looked thinner, sunken somehow, his eyes sunken into his head, his cheekbones riding high out of the gaunt flesh of his face. Wrinkles of loose flesh ridged at the base of his ear. I reached for Mary's hand.

She took my hand and murmured some sound of reassuring presence—Yes, I am here. Father's head moved slightly, and the gaunt arms stirred. He opened his eyes. Slowly, through a cloud, his eyes focused on us, and he saw us and smiled. "Hello, dear!"

"Hi, Father," I stooped to kiss him, to lay my face against his, my hand on his hand. "Mary, too," he said and reached toward her. His eyes moved back and forth between us, and he smiled again, taking us both in. He was fully awake now. "Well, when did you get here?" he asked slowly, the words following one another in an even progression, but thickly, almost as though each word must be formed in the throat, a conscious effort, then articulated.

"Last night, about ten, I guess."

"And Mary went down to get you?"

"Yes. Mary and Ed. I was coming from Chicago, you know."

"So Mother said. Did you have a good meeting?"

"Yes. Fine. A very good meeting." I looked at him. There was no censure from him, no note of reproach that I'd not

Spring 79

come sooner. Only that he looks wasted away—even the blue of his eyes seems paler, slightly opaque, the edges of his pupils less clearly defined. "How are you feeling, Father?" I did not ask him, How are you? Only, How are you feeling?

"Not too bad, I guess," he said, in a kind of contemplative and appraising way, his voice rising at the end, almost as though it was he who had asked the question.

We looked at each other for a moment—a recognition of his illness, of the presence and love of the three of us. "Well," he said, "tell me about Hoyt and the children."

I told him that Hoyt is fine and had been with me in Chicago and had now gone home to Tennessee, that Peter and John are fine in their colleges and will be getting out for the summer in another month, that Steve and Mary seem to be doing well in high school, and that, as he knows, Steve will be graduating in another month.

"And will go to Earlham in the fall?"

"Yes, that's his plan."

"Isn't that fine." His eyes stayed on us, affirming it all. Then he said, a kind of wistfulness in his voice, "How's Mother?"

"She seems OK. She sends her love. She'll be down this afternoon."

He closed his eyes, and a smile played across his lips. "She's glad to see you, I'm sure."

"Yes."

He turned again to Mary. "How are you, Mary dear?"

"Fine."

"Any word from Bruce and the children?"

"I talked to them on the phone last night. Jamesie's been sick for a couple of days, but he was back in school again. They're all fine."

"That's good," he said fondly. "Jamesie is quite a boy, isn't he?" James is the youngest of Mary's children. "Yes," she said. We talked on, about the children—Mary's and mine, about Esther's visit and Father's seeing Elizabeth and

Craig, and about a recent letter from Stephen. "They're having spring vacation soon," he said.

On the phone Stephen has told Mother he had planned to drive east this summer, as soon as school is out, and bring his family with him. Now he will not wait; he will fly east alone.

"Mother says Stephen may come later this week," I said.

"Yes," he said, and smiled again, some pleasant promise to himself that he may see his son again soon.

"And Mary's been here this week," he said, his eyes, grateful and acknowledging, on her. "I was glad to come," she said. The nod of her head was vigorous, assuring him many times over how glad she was to be here, how much she loves him.

His lips seem dry—he kept moistening them with his tongue.

"Would you like some ginger ale?" Mary asked. Since the beginning of his illness we have kept ginger ale in the hospital refrigerator for him.

"Mmm," he said, nodding.

"I'll get some," Mary said. She asked me, "Do you want to see where the refrigerator is?"

"Yes."

"We'll be back," she said to him.

We went out of the room, down the hallway to the small galley, and she showed me his several bottles of ginger ale—the brand he likes—and where the straws and the paper cups are kept. We poured him a cup.

For years ginger ale has been a favorite family beverage—first palliative for queasy stomachs, potion for easing toward recovery from childhood illness, base for ginger ale ice-cream sodas drunk around the family table on celebratory occasions late at night. It is all that, too, that we brought him, returning down the corridor with the fluted paper cup.

I offered it to him, holding the straw for him, and he pursed his lips and closed them and pulled up slowly on the amber liquid. His throat is so thin the sound of his swallow is like a knock—his Adam's apple jerking and falling. After the third drink he shook his head—he didn't want any more. I put the cup down.

He licked his lips again and gestured toward the bedside table. "Do you want the Carmex?" Mary asked. He nodded. She picked up a small jar of lip salve and took off the lid and held the jar for him. He took a little on a fingertip, spread it along his lips, and then nodded that he was finished, and she returned it to the table.

We sat in a broken silence, chatting idly from time to time—that it was a lovely day, that the spring flowers are blooming, and that soon it will be time for the boy to start mowing the lawn at home again. A nurse came in, straightened his covers, and asked if he needed anything. He smiled and shook his head no. Then he told her in his slow deliberate way that I am another one of his daughters, Mrs. Hickman, from Nashville, Tennessee. She smiled at me, and there was compassion in her eyes—I know why you have come and I am sorry. My eyes filled with tears, and I blinked them quickly away.

After a while, Mary and I acknowledged to each other that it was time to go. We said good-by to him and promised to come back with Mother in the afternoon. We went back into the hall, through the firedoors, and down in the elevator, out through the lobbies and reception room—too large, the spaces stretching out too far, with too few people inhabiting them—and to the car, in silence, the two of us together. In the car I asked, "Is that about how he's been?"

"Yes. Sometimes he's more alert than that, sometimes less so." We drove home, and to Mother's question, "How did you find Father?" I answered, "Not very good." She nodded and didn't say more.

In the afternoon we went back, three of us this time. In the doorway of his room we paused. He appeared to be asleep. His mouth was drooping open. Mother whispered, "Doesn't he look terrible?" We went into the room and distributed ourselves among the chairs and spaces. He woke again, slowly his eyes came into focus, and he greeted us. Mother said brightly, but with anxiety in her voice, "Well, how are you today, dear?"

"Not bad," he said and smiled at her. They talked about how nice it is to have Mary and me home and about the possibility that Stephen may come in several days. "Has the doctor been in today?" she asked.

"Not that I remember... though I suppose"—so slowly—"I could have been dozing."

On one occasion he started to cough, the cough struggling in his chest. He gestured toward a box of tissues on the bedside stand. Mary handed it to him. He took out a bunch and held it to his mouth and pulled away a heavy chain of phlegm. He dropped the tissues into a paper bag pinned to the side of his bed and lay back, exhausted.

The paper boy came with the afternoon paper. Mother got money from the bedside drawer and paid him. She asked Father if he wanted to look at the paper. "Guess not now," he said sleepily, and closed his eyes. The rest of us sat and read, passing sections of the paper back and forth, turning the pages slowly, and looking up from time to time to watch him as he lay there on the bed.

There was a jangling of food carts. A nurse came in bearing a supper tray—some soup, a stuffed pepper, applesauce, jello, bread, tea. She pulled his tray table over the bed. "Suppertime, Mr. Whitmore."

He opened his eyes. "So?" as though he was acknowledging the passing of the day.

The nurse offered him a small spoonful of soup. He shook his head—he didn't want any. She proffered bites of other things, and he tried a tiny mouthful or two, but then a look of distaste came on his face, and he shook his head.

Mother was on her feet beside him. "George, you've got to eat."

He took another bite, refused the next. She persisted, scolding, "Do you want to get sicker?"

"No." His voice was strong with a hint of anger, and I cringed, thinking, *How can she ask him such a question?* But I know she is desperate and doesn't know what to do with her need. He ate a few more bites and drank some tea, then shook his head—No more. The nurse left, and his head sank further into the pillow.

We gathered up our things. Mary and I told him we'd be back this evening.

"When is it you go back to Appleton, Mary?" His voice was guarded, a yearning in it.

"Tomorrow afternoon."

"You'll be in, in the morning?"

"Yes."

We kissed him good-by and left.

At supper it was what we talked about—how he seems, that he doesn't want to eat, that he coughs, that he dozes off so much but is at other times very alert. We wonder how long he can live, as low as he is. It has seemed to me, watching the rise and fall of his chest, that his breathing is very rapid—I suppose he is compensating for the uselessness of one lung. He is surely terribly weak. Mother said, anticipating Mary's return to Appleton tomorrow, "In a few days you'll just have to turn around and come back."

In the evening, he scarcely noticed Mary and me. Once or twice he came up from drowsiness to smile at us, his eyes lighting up, almost in their old way. Then he subsided back into sleep. We stayed until we heard the nurses on their bedtime rounds. He would be settling for the night soon, whatever that means for him—whatever he perceives of the patterns of day and night, of lights coming and going, of sounds changing, and of food or its absence marking the hours of the time that is passing. We kissed him good night and, so sweetly, he smiled at us, his eyes closed.

Back at the house, Mother had had a phone call from Stephen. His courses will be over Friday, and he will come. A friend will oversee the giving of his exams. He'll let us know later the exact time of his arrival.

May 8. This morning when Mary and I visited Father he was very alert—brightly awake when we arrived, full of cheer. He had slept well. He told us in detail, bragging, how much breakfast he had eaten, elaborating on each item. The nurses had been in and bathed him. He felt pretty good.

We told him—especially glad to tell him on this day when Mary is leaving—that Stephen called last night and will be coming Friday. His cheer increased. He talked on with Mary, mindful that she would be going.

He has said nothing to any of us about his general appraisal of his condition. I wonder, *Does he still hope to get well?* Seeing him this morning, one could almost believe it possible. We had a lovely visit, laughing and joking some, and shortly before lunch Mary and I left, promising to drop by for a few moments in the early afternoon on our way to the airport.

We went home and ate lunch with Mother. Mary assembled her luggage, and we put it in the car.

At the hospital we parked the car and went in, the air between us heavy with sadness. After today she will not see him again. We went to Father's room. He was asleep. I waited by the door. Mary went to the side of the bed. "Father." He opened his eyes and smiled but scarcely seemed to see that it was she, or even that a person stood there waiting. "I'm going," she said. He made some low sound of response, but his eyelids were closed again. She stooped to kiss him, and for a second I closed my eyes. She stood beside him, looking down, then started to walk away from him toward the door, but turned back. "I want to kiss him again," she said and went back and stooped over him again. I stood in the cloud of sorrow that filled the room and wondered that we have come to this place—all of us who lived in the house and joined our lives together in childhood, in adolescence, in maturity, in sickness and in health, in nearness and in distance, and in a love that is, at the end, without a name, except that perhaps today it is his name—Father—and he is dying. She moved away from him and, turning, we went out into the hall. "I don't think he knew I was leaving," she said. "Maybe it's just as well."

We drove to the airport and kissed each other good-by, and she went—we knew we would see each other again soon.

When I got back from the airport, Mother and I went to the hospital. Father was much more alert. He spoke of Mary's having gone but said nothing of our dropping by earlier in the afternoon. He spoke of Stephen's coming Friday.

At one point he asked how my novel is coming. I told him I'm nearing the end of it—that I have, in fact, brought along a few more chapters in case Mother has any inclination to read them. He misunderstood, thinking I had the manuscript with me at the hospital. "Well, shall we read some of it now?"

I was touched at his asking. It saddens me to know he will never read this work when it is finished, though he has read some of it. It saddens me partly because the work is so much about the influences and uses of the past and because he looms so large in my own past. It saddens me because he has been so pleased at every success of mine and I shall miss his pride in me.

"Oh, it's at the house, not here." Anyway, I'm sure it would tire him and embarrass me, to read aloud from it for long.

"Well, then," he said, "tell me some more about Hoyt and his work." That I can do.

Later in our visit, Mother and I were looking at the afternoon paper, and I asked if he'd like me to read any of it to him. He thought for a minute, then said with a smile, "Tell me how the Red Sox are doing." I turned to the sports page and found an account of yesterday's game. "The Red Sox won!" I read down the columns to find their standing in the league. He is pleased they are doing so well.

As I turned back to the paper, I remembered Saturday afternoons with the family radio turned to the Red Sox game and Father coming in from working in the yard to listen a few minutes and catch up on the score. I remember the summer day he took Stephen to Boston to a World

Series game in which the Red Sox were playing and how excited the whole family was at their going. I remember an interlude of several days one summer when only my father and I were at home and our dinner conversations always included some drillwork for me, which my father conducted in a half-serious, half-joking way on the makeup of the two major leagues. "American League... Boston Red Sox, New York Yankees, Cleveland Indians...; National League... St. Louis Cardinals, Chicago Cubs, Pittsburgh Pirates..." By the time the rest of the family came home I had memorized them all. I forgot them soon enough (though my loyalty to the Red Sox remains absolute) but never the fun we had going through it all—my father at least half-caring that I know, for the information's sake, and I going along gladly but only for the ritual and repartee between us as I recited my way through the lists. "American League... Boston Red Sox..."

The supper trays came. I offered to feed him. He wanted to know what was on the tray—soup, a ground meat dish, beans, bread, tea, some ice cream that was already beginning to melt.

"I'll try the meat," he said, and bite by agonizing bite he ate the whole serving, stopping from time to time to ask how much was left, like a runner appraising the distance he has yet to go. At the end of it he sank back, exhausted from the effort. He didn't want anything else, not even the tea, and when I offered to get some ginger ale, no, he didn't want that, either. But he was proud of his accomplishment. I'm sure he forced himself to eat that much and chose the meat, thinking it would give him strength. Could the doctor be wrong—might he, just possibly, grow strong again?

In the evening when I went up he slept most of the time. When he did speak, his voice was thick and barely audible.

He heard the nurses going on their bedtime rounds, and he wished they would get to him, so he could settle for the night. Would I look and see if they were coming? He seemed restless even in his semitorpor. I went to the hallway and looked up the corridor. A nurse was carrying fresh linen into a room four doors away. "They're working toward us," I said.

"Maybe they do the sickest ones last." It was a murmur only and I thought, *Yes, he knows how sick he is.* When the nurse came, I told her how eager he was to get to sleep. I kissed him. "Good-by, dear. I'll see you tomorrow."

What we have waited for....

May 9. This morning early we put in a call to the hospital—we'd like to talk with the doctor. Could he call back? The nurse said she'd tell him. He called soon. I talked with him. I told him I was one of Mr. Whitmore's daughters, and I was here from Tennessee. I knew my father's condition was critical. Could he tell me any more? I was going to have to go back in a few days—did he have any idea how long my father might live?

The voice on the other end of the line was kind—speaking in an accent whose origin I did not recognize. He'd seen Father yesterday, he told me—he was a very sick man. It was, in a way, surprising he had lived this long. "He has a strong constitution." Perhaps I could stay a few more days? I told him I'd be here until Sunday, but my brother was coming on Friday so there'd be someone here with my mother. He'd wanted to ask, he said, whether we all wanted to be there at the end. Not necessarily, I said, though we certainly wanted at least one of us. We didn't want our father—or mother—to be alone. He wondered about our religion—did our religion call for any final prayers or ceremonies? I said no, we were Protestant, we had no last rites of the church. My father—I felt compelled to tell the doctor—had been a very good man, had lived a good life. We felt no need of any particularized ritual to sanction his leaving life. "Yes," the doctor said. "Yes. I can tell he is a good man, he is really a wonderful fellow." He promised to call if there was anything else we should know. I thanked him, and we said good-by. I reported the conversation to Mother before I set out for the hospital.

Father was groggy when I got here, but he comes to alertness from time to time, to chat with me a few minutes, then falls back into sleep...

I sat in the chair in the corner of his room and, turning the pages in a haze of not seeing, I glanced through the morning paper I found unopened on his stand. I put the paper down and sat quietly, watching him. From time to time a frown creased his forehead. Occasionally he shifted his position, though for any major change in his body now the nurses have to move him—he is too weak to turn from one side to the other. His body is wraithlike. His arms lie against his body like angled sticks, and on one wrist the white plastic identification bracelet rises in a hoop.

His face, too, is diminished. The bone of his nose is a sharp ridge—it has never been so. His mouth is sunken in. He has worn dentures for fifteen years, but until these last weeks we have never seen him without them—he is proud. Now he is too thin, the teeth cannot stay in place, they are put away. His face is transformed, and yet it is he. There is life in him.

I got up from the chair and laid my hand on his forehead, and he smiled, though he did not open his eyes. He is warm and present to us—for how much longer? I stooped to lay my cheek against his—to comfort him? to comfort myself? to hope that, by osmosis, my energy would pass to him, my love revive him? I sat down in the chair again and picked up the paper, but I did not read.

There is a strange comfort in being with him, as though all else gathers here and is still. When he is drowsing, it is all right. When he is awake, it is affirming, too. This is where reality waits and rests its case.

This afternoon was, I guess, what I have wanted—both dreaded and wanted—and now that it has come and the unspoken has been spoken, we can only wait as in some holy present for what else may come. I am grateful for Father and for his clarity, and that he seems to have passed some milestone in his life's adventure, and so have we all.

We are here, and the resolution is occurring, gravely, as though somehow it stands alone, he stands alone, as though we have nothing to offer except our love which presses so fiercely upon him, which loves but cannot keep him.

This afternoon Mother and I went to the hospital as we've been doing, and we each took our place on chairs at either side of his bed. We chatted some and sat in silence some. He was lying back against the pillow, going in and out of drowsiness as he has been doing.

At one point he asked me whether the doctor had been in today—in his state of grogginess he often does not remember. I said I didn't know, but if he'd like me to I would ask the nurse. Yes, he indicated, he would. So I went out into the hall and asked the nurse. She said no, the doctor had not been in today, but he would be here tomorrow. I went back and sat down and told Father what the nurse had said—that the doctor had not been here today but would be tomorrow.

Then, his eyes still closed, he said, in the same slow, matter-of-fact way in which he's been speaking, "Not to me."

"Not to you?"

"I won't be here," he said, slowly again, simply, into the air of a room suddenly filled with—what? angels? portents? the sudden banishment of tables and chairs and coats and trays, leaving only some terrible energy of truth, at last located and addressed? I stood up to lean over him. "Father!"

I looked over to Mother to see if she had heard. She was looking up, alarmed at my sudden rising, her eyes questioning—what's the matter?

"He said he won't be here tomorrow," I said. Comprehending instantly, she got up from her chair and leaned over him. "Darling!" she said—an outpouring of fifty years of shared life spilling over him as he lay there on the bed, telling us his truth.

He went on: "I won't be here in the morning." We waited, speechless, motionless, struck with it. Then Mother said, "Would you like Martha and me to say the 'Our

Father'?" His eyes still closed, he nodded—yes—and she began, and together she and I went through the familiar words—a kind of groping, I suppose, for some ritual of belief and hope to hold to when the world seems falling away. I thought, grateful to her, *Yes, it is the right thing to be doing*—for it was a risk I wouldn't have taken, but now, saying the words together, they seemed to ring clear, reverberating through our need like a bell.

We finished, and there was a kind of holy silence. Then Father went on deliberately, "If I don't wake up, give my blessings to all my friends and children and grandchildren," and, not knowing what to say, I said, "Father, you *are* the blessing." I thought of them all—Mary, Stephen, Esther, all of us, wives and husbands gathered around, and our children, from young men and women to two-year-old Elizabeth—a company of loved ones, and in an impulse to preserve the moment for them, and also because I am a writer and a moment so grave and holy should not pass unrecorded, I reached for a paper and pen and wrote down the words he had said—"For the others," I said to Mother, and she nodded.

Father was speaking again, the same measured tones, his eyes still closed. "Thank the nurses," he said. He paused, as though contemplating. "The doctor said I was a strong man." He seemed to smile ruefully to himself. He waited a minute, then said, "I may be here longer, but I think it's coming overnight."

I wondered, *What does he see?* What intimations of presence wait in the shadows ready or not? And I saw him in the night, waiting, wondering as he felt himself grow sleepy ... "I won't wake up in the morning." Or is he too sick for all that, and will he go to sleep mindlessly, a simple dropping away, a laying it all to rest?

The silence waited. I, too, must speak. My heart raced. My father would never go out on such a limb. It is against the family pattern of reserve, of not making overly ambitious statements. But—it mattered with a terrible intensity. I said, "I believe that we shall know each other again."

Father's eyebrows lifted, the corners of his mouth turned down a little, he raised his hands, turning his forearms slightly to the outside. It was a gesture of—Who knows? —and he was proclaiming himself again. He would not for himself or me affirm anything he feels is such a mystery as whether any of us shall survive death. He had declared himself, and I had declared myself, and it was good. In silence we waited again, and in the room with us waited an immeasurable closeness—we are a part of one another, except that he will go and leave us here. What shall we do with the life space that has been his, when he is gone? The void of his passing hovers, and all of us know it and wonder.

After a while the suppers came. He let me feed him a few mouthfuls of soup and jello. He has no interest in food.

We knew a guest waited for us at home. Mother had invited a woman who has helped during times of illness in the past and who has become a close family friend. She would be waiting. She would have set the table in readiness.

But we didn't want to leave Father for two hours—if he feels death close, he needs someone with him. "Why don't I take you home," I suggested to Mother. "Then I'll come back."

She demurred for a moment—she was reluctant to leave him, but realized the limitations of her strength, and that the friend would be waiting. "All right." We consulted him. That would be fine. We kissed him good-by and left.

In the hall we told the nurse of Father's premonition he will die in the night. Her expression changed; she was subdued and compassionate. Was it her experience, we wondered, that such premonitions are usually borne out?

Often they are not, she said. Sometimes a patient will feel that way and then live on for days or even weeks. But sometimes they are. You can't know. We nodded and thanked her. I told her I was taking my mother home and would be back.

In the car we were silent for a while in the face of what had happened. Then we talked, wondering whether we should call the others, wondering whether his premonition is true, and he may die in the night.

Mary has just been here. Stephen is coming Friday. Esther has spoken of coming right after Roy's birthday next week. For months she's been planning a surprise party for his fortieth birthday. Friends are coming from far and near, the neighbor's freezer is full of food. Of course she could cancel the party and come, and she may have to do that anyway...if Father dies. But if they can have their party, their gathering of friends, we want them to. I remember my ambivalence about the Chicago meeting. Their party will help them with what is to come.

We decided to wait—it would take them many hours to reach here and if his intuition of himself is true, they would be too late. When we do talk with them, we'll tell them of the conversation. In a way they will be relieved. The bridge of silence has been crossed. They, too, have been waiting.

When we arrived at home, Mrs. Cox was waiting. She was grieved and full of sympathy. She, marvelous guest that she is, had finished getting the supper. She and Mother would eat. I'd go, and if later on Father should appear to be settled for a long night's sleep, I might come back.

I left them and returned to the hospital. Father was asleep, his face calm and untroubled. I sat down and got out a book and began to read. I was content, grateful that I could be here. The cord of tension that stretches from him on the bed and reaches to wherever I am, to the awareness of him that stays with me now every waking hour, is relaxed and at peace when I am with him.

A nurse came in—the same nurse Mother and I talked with in the hall. She wondered if she could bring me something to eat? The nurses are making hero sandwiches for themselves and they have lots of extra—they'd be glad to fix one for me. Why, yes, I would like that very much, that's very good of them. Do I like tomato? onion? salami? lettuce? cheese? Yes, all those things. Would I like a Pepsi? Yes, thank you.

She left and returned with the tray and handed it to me. I

received it, grateful for the food and for the caring that rose like the bubbles from the dark liquid in the glass.

I stayed on. Visitors came and went through the hall. Nurses prepared patients for the night. The hospital fell silent again.

The nursing shift changed. I heard talking in the hall and heard Father's name.

It was late when a nurse came in and said, "Why don't you go? We'll be giving him his medicine, and he'll probably sleep through the night."

I was tired but loathe to leave him. "You have our telephone number?"

She nodded.

"You'll call us if there's any change?"

"Yes."

"Perhaps I'll go then." I knew Mother would be anxious to see me. I was desperately tired. I went over and stood by him and put my hand on his. He did not stir or appear to notice me. "He'll probably hardly wake for the medicine, then he'll go right back to sleep," the nurse said.

"You'll call me, even if he's just restless?"

"Yes."

I stooped to kiss him and lay my cheek on his forehead, savoring his reality—that there was life in him yet—frail, flickering, sifting away. But still, the life that has carried him for eighty years inhabits his body at this moment. The unknown country of death is not entered yet. Good night, Father. Good night. Whenever it is, good night.

He is still here. Mother falls....

May 10. The hospital didn't call in the night, but something else happened, adding its ironic complications to our lives. In the night Mother fell in the bathroom, hitting her hip hard against the bathroom scale, knocking her head against the towel rack. Hearing the crash, I rushed in from my room to find her sitting on the floor, her back against the wall. "Well! Will you look at what I just did!" she said, impatience and consternation in her voice.

"Are you all right?"

"I think so. I don't think I broke anything. I gave my hip a pretty good whack against the scale." The scale was between her body and the edge of the bathtub.

"Do you think you can get up?"

"Yes. Give me your hand."

I reached down and slowly helped her to a standing position. "How does it feel?"

"It's sore, but I don't think I broke anything." Slowly we walked together back to her bedroom, and I helped her into bed. "Do you think you'll be able to go back to sleep?"

"I think so."

"We'll see how it is in the morning, OK?"

"Yes." I kissed her good night again and went back to my room and got into bed. My heart was racing, and I was wide awake. What next? I thought of Father—the hospital hadn't called us. In the morning we'd probably have to call the doctor about Mother. The responsibility of being the only well person here and of dealing with all of this seems almost more than I can handle. I'm glad Stephen is coming in a few days.

After what seemed like hours, I went back to sleep.

Mother was stiff and sore when she woke up, but was able to get up and to the bathroom. I brought her breakfast on a tray, and while she was eating I called the hospital...

"How is Mr. Whitmore?"

"He is resting comfortably. There has been no change."

I explained to the nurse on duty about my mother's fall. I would get there as soon as I could.

I helped Mother call Dr. Calhoun. He wanted her to have an X ray; he would send an ambulance. I helped her into her robe. In a few minutes the ambulance came, and the men came up the stairs and began to prepare her for the journey, wrapping her hair in a dark green cloth, laying her carefully on the stretcher, covering her body with green blankets, and fastening straps across her chest and legs to keep her from slipping. By the time we got downstairs, Francine and Mr. Adams, neighbors from next door and across the street, were at the open door. They'd seen the ambulance.

I explained. Then Francine stood with me as Mother was carried down the stairs. We held our breath as the men raised the stretcher to clear the bannister—and Mother's head all but grazed the sloping ceiling of the stairwell. "You OK?" I called.

"I'm fine," she called back.

The men put her in the ambulance. I followed in the car. In case she had to be admitted, I'd need the car to return home.

In the hospital corridor we waited. "Why did I have to go and do a thing like this!" she exclaimed. Yet it almost seemed to have energized her. I recall as a child sightseeing in Washington in unbearable heat; I fell and cut my knee on the sidewalk, and it was almost a relief—something else to think about but the heat.

The orderlies wheeled her in for an X ray. I waited, thinking, *If she has broken a hip she'll have to stay here for weeks, and Father will die, and she won't even be able to go to the funeral. We'll all have to go away and leave her in the hospital. Or perhaps I could have her flown to a nursing home in Nashville for convalescence, or Esther or Stephen or Mary could...* And my thoughts echoed her own words, *Why did she have to go and do a thing like this?* And I realized that in the strange protective mechanisms of the body, maybe now was just the time for her to take such a fall—now, when Father's death was so imminent, the long strand of her courage and fortitude was breaking, and she couldn't take it any more, and she fell.

A technician brought the X-ray report. She has broken nothing. She has a bad bruise. Except for going to the bathroom, she should stay off her feet for twenty-four hours. She'll be stiff and sore for several weeks, but it's all right for her to walk.

Mother was brought back. I leaned to embrace her. "Well, that's good news, dear!"

"We didn't need that, did we?" She smiled, obviously relieved.

The ambulance brought her home. The men put her on the daybed in the dining room. She can sleep down here without having to navigate the stairs to go to bed. With the help of her cane and my arm, she can get to the bathroom, though every step brings a sharp intake of breath.

As soon as she was settled, I left to see Father. I didn't want to leave him alone with his unfulfilled prophecy. The thought occurred to me, *Is he embarrassed, not to have died?* My need to be with him was almost panic.

He was asleep when I got there, but wakened. He looks as he did yesterday—if the angel of death had come closer in the night I could see no sign.

"Well, Marthy, I'm still here," Father said and smiled wanly.

"Yes, dear." I held my hand over his, absorbing his presence. How can I but be glad? "The doctor told us you had a strong constitution," I said, remembering.

"Oh? When was that?"

Was it only yesterday? It seems ages ago. "Yesterday morning."

"What else did he say?"

"He said you are a wonderful fellow."

He smiled.

"Father," I said, after a moment, "Mother fell in the night."

"Oh?" He was alarmed.

I told him the circumstances and that she has broken no bones, but is very sore and must stay quiet for twenty-four hours. He asked a few questions, pressing for details. "She won't come this afternoon, but she said she'll try to come tomorrow," I said. He nodded, registering nothing but acceptance.

"How are you feeling?" I asked.

"About the same." His voice was resigned and quiet. He rubbed his hand over his chest. The nurse came in to move him to his other side. She slid her arms under his body and cupped her hands around him and he turned, all of a piece, light, frail, his elbows close to his sides. "Is that all right, Mr. Whitmore?" He smiled and nodded—yes. His eyes were closed.

A tray of lunch came—clear soup, jello, tea. Nothing to build a body back to strength. "Can I feed you?" He opened his mouth dutifully for a few bites, then shook his head—that's all.

"Can I get you some ginger ale?"

"No, thank you, dear. I quess not."

The nurse returned for the tray. "He didn't want very much," I said. She nodded. "We'll bring him some juice after a while." A grimace crossed his face, and he swallowed hard.

"I'm going to the house," I said. "I'll get some lunch for Mother and me and be back this afternoon."

"That's fine, dear...." He opened his eyes—they are clear, and a look of understanding and compassion flowed from them, and I stooped to lay my cheek on his. "Father!" He pressed my hand. I stood up. "I'll be back this afternoon." He nodded, his eyes closed again.

In the afternoon he was much the same, coming and going out of drowsiness. At one point he said, as though talking out into the air, though I knew it was to me, "I don't suppose the grandchildren will be able to come...such a long way, so expensive." To his funeral was what he meant, though he didn't say so. I said, "I don't know, Father. It is a long way." Hoyt and I have already talked over the phone about our children—if they want to come and school is not too pressing, we'll gladly finance the trip—we'll leave it up to them.

Late in the afternoon a priest came in, a white-haired man with a kind face. I hadn't met him before, but he seemed to know Father. He came to the side of the bed and after asking Father how he was feeling today, he said to me in a gravelly, matter-of-fact voice, "He likes to have me pray with him." He began his prayer, and I bowed my head but with a touch of anger intruding—*He is not an object. Why are you talking about him when he is here?*

You are angry at life, I told myself, *for taking your father away.*

In a few minutes the priest left. "He's a nice man," Father said.

"Yes."

In the middle of the afternoon I got some ginger ale and offered it to Father. He took a long draw, and the liquid rose halfway up the straw and dropped down again—he didn't have the strength to pull it all the way up. A nurse came. "Here, let me show you." She dropped the straw into the glass, then holding her fingertip over the end of the straw to keep the liquid from escaping, she lifted the straw to his lips and released her finger, letting the ginger ale flow into his mouth.

"Thank you." I took it from her and gave him several more drinks, until he moved his head away—he didn't want any more.

"Try and get him to drink the liquid," the nurse said. "He needs that."

After a while a nurse brought supper—ice cream, jello, tea. "You'll have to help him with it," she said. "He's gotten to the place where someone has to feed him. He hasn't the strength to feed himself."

After the nurse left he said, "What did she say?"

I repeated her words. "Is that all?" he asked.

"Yes." I offered him a few bites of the food. He took a little of the jello, but that was all. "Marthy," he said, speaking softly, his eyes closed. "There isn't any doubt that it's cancer, is there?"

I said, the words catching in my throat, but thinking, the truth—this is the time for no word but the truth—"No, Father, there's no doubt. The doctor said 'malignant thymoma.' "

He nodded, accepting the words. "I wondered a little about emphysema," he said.

"I haven't heard anybody say that," I said. He started to cough as though he would strangle, and I held a tissue to his mouth to pull out the heavy fluid that came from his lung. The cough subsided, and he nodded and fell back onto the pillow.

Emphysema. The specter of tobacco. I was an adolescent before I knew my father smoked. "It was a present he gave me, of a clean house," my mother said, explaining why (I forget how I had learned) my father smoked at the office but never at home. He had started to smoke in the army. When they married, she had wanted him to quit. "I was terribly hurt that he wouldn't," she said, "that he wouldn't do it for me." She paused. "He almost felt it a point of honor, not to quit for that reason." At the time I felt the pain of it. I feel it again now. My father has not smoked in recent years.

A few minutes later I told him I was going back to the house—I'd be here again after supper.

While I was at the hospital this evening Francine came in. She and Ed have lived next door to Mother and Father for only a few years, but they have been warm friends from the start. Francine, who is a nurse, bent over Father with the tenderness of a daughter. I could see she was checking his pulse, watching his respiration rate even as she talked, telling him how the neighbors kept asking for him, telling him she had seen Mother and, despite her fall, Mother was doing well, telling him what a sweet fellow he is and how they miss him on the street. After we had both kissed him good night and were walking down the corridor, I asked her if she had any idea how much longer he might live. "Not more than a few days I would think, Martha," she said. "He is very poor." In the parking lot we got into our separate cars and drove home.

Stephen comes....

May 11. This morning before breakfast I called the hospital to ask about Father. "His condition is poor," the nurse said. "But there is no change since yesterday. He is resting quietly."

It is very difficult for Mother to get around, but she is going to try to go to the hospital this afternoon. This morning I went up—no particular change. At one point a nurse brought some fruit juice and was urging Father to drink some. "I don't see why," he said, an edge of complaint in his voice. "It'll only keep me here longer." The nurse took in the words, almost an accusation. "It's to keep you comfortable, Mr. Whitmore," and I thought, *Thank you, for telling him the truth*—no mythology about making you strong, helping you get better. He acknowledged her words and opened his lips to receive another drink.

I took Mother this afternoon—brought a hospital wheelchair out to the car, and then to Father's room. He was all commiseration for her fall, and yet I feel it does not enter that deeply into his consciousness—as though when one is about to die, a bruised hipbone is regrettable but of no great consequence—or as though what he can share with us has somehow grown shallower, thinned down, he is so much about his own business now, which is to get on with dying.

We reminded him that Stephen will be here in time for an evening visit, and then I told him what I have dreaded telling him, that in two days, on Sunday, I shall be going back to Tennessee.

I told him why—that Mary, our daughter, has an appointment with the orthopedic surgeon. We have recently discovered a slight spinal curvature. The surgeon has taken X rays. We are to go back on Monday. If the curvature has increased, she must start wearing a body brace from her hips to her chin, "until she stops growing." The prospect of encasing her beautiful young woman's body in a clumsy thickening brace now that she is fifteen and so acutely aware of her appearance brings a knot to the pit of my stomach. If that is to be the doctor's prescription on Monday, I want to be there with her.

I told him this, and he nodded—he understands. "Thank you for coming, dear," he said, his voice stretched out over the silence.

Late this afternoon Stephen came. He'd suggested on the phone that I not leave Holyoke to come to the airport to meet him. He'd take the bus, get to the house himself. About five the doorbell rang. I went to the door. At the sight of him—tall, strong, healthy—I felt some box of control, of trying to be adequate, give way, and I put my arms around his chest and clung to him, sobbing. For several minutes we stood in the doorway embracing one another. "Is it that bad, dear?" he asked softly.

Then we went back into the dining room where Mother was lying on the daybed. With his coming there is someone else to share the grief and responsibility. I feel immeasurable eased.

After supper we went to see Father. I had thought perhaps Stephen would prefer to go alone, but he wanted me to come with him. On the way I said, "He looks terrible" —to prepare him, if anything can, if there is any preparation, ever.

We went to the door of the room. Father's face was turned toward us, his mouth sunken, his ears too big, now that his face seems smaller. The light shone on his silver-gray hair. He appeared asleep. But when Stephen went over and spoke his name—"Father!"—he stirred and opened his eyes and light came into them, and he smiled a broad smile of welcome. "Steve!" he said, and reached his hand up as my brother stooped to kiss him, then stood again as they savored the presence of each other.

After a while Father said, "I didn't think I'd still be here, Steve," a kind of wondering in his voice—the puzzlement as to how it could be. "I know," my brother said, and they were silent again. "How are you feeling? Are you comfortable?"

"Reasonably so—a little uneasy, here and there." Father passed his hand over his chest and shifted his shoulder ever so slightly against the sheet.

"Do you want me to move you?" Stephen asked.

"Guess not, thanks," Father said, and then began to ask about Stephen's family—how they all were.

"Fine. They send their love." He went on to tell some anecdotes about the children—how Daniel, who had broken his arm in a fall, was getting along with his cast, how Michael was playing in Little League, and how Sarah had started piano lessons. Father lay still throughout this recitation. Watching him I thought, *He is bathed in gladness. He is happy. Even under these circumstances, he is happy.*

After we'd stayed a while longer we both kissed him good night, promised to see him in the morning, and went back to the house.

Mother asked Stephen, "Well, how did he seem to you?"

"Not very good. But better than I thought he might. He was very alert, asking about the family, talking with us."

"It revives him to have Steve here," I said.

Mr. Jackson comes. . . .

May 12. This morning Father was very alert again. He asked Steve to shave him. He drank some ginger ale. He spoke again, in a kind of wonderment, of the fact that he was still alive. There was almost something of the old jokester in him. When Stephen said, "The doctor told us you had a strong constitution," Father said wryly, "I thought as much," and then added, with the old lift in his voice, in a paraphrase of the doctor's compliment, "And an admirable personality."

He was quiet for a while, and when he spoke he was serious again. "I keep thinking," he said, "that some time I'll go to sleep and not wake up again." And my brother, my angel brother, stood by the bed and leaned over him, his broad shoulders coming between my father and the light. "That will happen sometime, Dad. But we'll be with you until it does." And my father nodded and smiled and was at rest.

Late this afternoon, after the three of us had come from the hospital and were having a cup of tea, Mr. Jackson, the minister of the other Baptist church in town and a long-time family friend, dropped in to see Mother. He came back to the dining room and took her hand, kissed her cheek and, at our urging, pulled up a chair to have tea with us.

"I was just up to see George," he said to Mother. "I thought I'd stop by and see you, too. He said you'd fallen."

"Yes." She explained the circumstances. He inquired how all of us were and chatted with my brother, whom he'd not met before.

"How did you think George was?" Mother asked him.

"Not good."

"He's talked about dying, you know," she said.

He nodded. "I know." He was quiet for a minute. Then he began, "I said to him, 'You know we love you and Ruth.' And you know what he said?"

"What?" She is alert for any word.

"He said, 'That's right—love Ruth.'"

"Did he?" Her voice rose in a kind of glad surprise. "That's nice to remember, isn't it?" She looked at Stephen and me, and there were tears in her eyes—she who does not often cry. "'Love Ruth'"—she said the words again softly—a gift from Father to her.

"I wanted to tell you," Mr. Jackson said. "That's one reason I came." He rose to go. "Call me if you need me." He clasped her hand again, nodded to us, and was gone.

We sat in the dining room together, grateful for the visit, and for Father, reaching out across his dying—since he knew how she needed love and he would soon be gone.

Uncle Harold had asked that I call before I go back to Tennessee, to tell him how Father is. I called tonight at six, and he answered the phone. He was wondering whether to come up or not—Would Father know he was here? Sometimes he might, I said, and often he would not—he is very groggy much of the time, though he seems to have revived a bit with Stephen here. But much of the time he doesn't seem to know who's there or what's happening.

"I don't especially want to come," Uncle Harold said, "if it isn't going to make any difference to him that I'm there." We agree that it is problematical—chances are that Father would scarcely notice. He will not come now, then, but will plan to come for the funeral, whenever that is. He sends us his love. He is a comfort, four hundred miles away. We shall call him, when the time comes.

This is my last night here. Going to bed I wonder, as I have each night of this visit, whether he may die in the night and this part of it will be over and we shall get on with the rest of it.

This is also the night of Esther's surprise party for Roy. Tomorrow we'll call them—maybe they can come. Stephen said to me, "What shall I do when you're gone?" Knowing how hard it was for me before he came—particularly after Mother fell and has had such pain and needs so much help getting around—I hope Esther can come for a while, though I know she couldn't stay indefinitely. Stephen has a three-week break now, between semesters, so he can stay.

I wonder if I should stay longer myself and ask Hoyt to go with Mary to find out about the brace. But I want to be with her. And, yes, there is a way in which I want to leave this place for a while—it is too hard, and I crave the presence of my husband and children, for stability, for comfort. Yet I am loathe to leave my father, and I wonder that death takes such a long time to come. I know we have much to be grateful for—particularly that Father doesn't appear to be suffering, except from weakness.

Does the knowledge of the ebbing away of life cause him anguish? To us who are strong, whose senses are acutely open to the mystery and wonder of life, the dying of sense seems an affront beyond consolation. Is it an affront to him, too, or does he wait for it, floating back on it, as one lies on water? I remember once waking from surgery and feeling nothing but overwhelming weakness, as though to lift my hand would require all my available power. I had no energy, or even interest, for sustained speculation about myself, and I wondered, as a thought drifting by, whether dying was like that. Only to me, strength returned and to him it will not, and that is an unbridgeable ocean. We cannot be where he is. We cannot feel it, or endure it, or make it other than it is—except that our love and presence matter to him and help him. But the burden of it is his, and no attempted possessiveness of ours, no projection of the will or encompassing cloud of sympathy, can take it from him. That, too, is hard to accept, when our love would uphold him with strong ropes if it could.

Tomorrow, in the middle of the afternoon, I shall go home.

Leaving. . . .

May 13. This morning Stephen and I went to the hospital a little earlier than usual because this is the day of my going. It is a prospect who can bear? When we got there the door to Father's room was closed, and I thought, my heart in my throat, *Has it come?* But no, the nurse came out and said they were bathing him and changing his linen. It would be about half an hour before he was ready for visitors.

Stephen suggested we go for a ride, and we drove out from the city, along some of the roads we used to take on Sunday afternoon family drives—past the reservoir and Ashley Ponds and Clayton's Beach. New vacation houses have sprung up along the shores, but the lakes are unchanged—sandy beaches on the side nearest the road and across the lakes a shoreline of dark pine trees. We got lost on some of the unfamiliar turns of road, but found our way again and came back to the hospital. This time the door of his room was open, and we went in.

He lay there looking wasted and old, his chest rising and

falling. He looked at us and smiled weakly, and some unintelligible word of greeting came from his throat. We asked him the questions—How are you feeling? Are you comfortable? Can I get you a drink of something? To all of these he answered with a slight motion of the head or a faint lift of the brows. We told him we planned to call Esther this afternoon. We told him that Mother sent her love and that she was doing all right, though it hurt her to walk, but she planned to come this afternoon. He seemed to hear us, but he didn't speak. We told him we'd been here earlier, but the door was closed. They were readying him for the day.

Then because I must, I said, calling to him through the cloud of his weakness and apparent drowsiness, "Father, I am going back to Tennessee this afternoon."

He nodded slowly but said nothing. I stood by his bed, my hand on his, stooping to kiss him from time to time or lay my cheek against his forehead, and all the while he didn't speak, but lay with eyes closed, seeming to drift in and out of our presence.

It was getting on toward lunchtime, and I said, again through the soundless and invisible barrier of his condition, calling to him in his apparent remoteness, "Father, we're going to the house now. We'll be back this afternoon."

His lips began to move, working from the corners, and his eyes still closed, his head motionless, he said in a clear voice, "How soon?"

Startled, I looked at Stephen. "As soon as we can," I said.

We had lunch, and I finished packing. Before we left to go to the hospital we called Esther. How was the birthday party?

It had been a wonderful success. Friends had amassed at a neighbor's house and paraded up the street, singing and shouting and blowing party horns. Yes, Roy was surprised. They'd all had a marvelous time. The house had been crowded, but no one seemed to mind. She was tired and jubilant in the aftermath of the successful party. How, she wondered, was Father?

We told her of his worsening condition, his premonition about dying. Could she possibly come? Steve was still here, of course, but I was leaving.

She was full of compassion for the situation, touched and grateful that we'd waited until the party was over. Yes, she was sure they could come. She'd talk with Roy. She couldn't leave the babies or drive with them alone—probably they'd all come. Roy could bring work with him to do in Holyoke. She'd call back and let us know when they'd be arriving.

Relieved, the three of us—Mother and Stephen and I—prepared to leave for the hospital. Stephen put my suitcase in the car. He'd take me from the hospital to the airport. Mother would stay with Father until he returned.

We arrived at the hospital, got a wheelchair for Mother, and together went to his room.

He was groggy again, but acknowledged by some slow sound of "hello," some motion of a hand, that he knew we were there. The words coming thick like a broken chain of cotton, he asked Mother how she was. She was doing all right, she said. She asked how he felt and speculated on whether the doctor had come in.

We offered him drinks of water. We told him we'd called Esther, the party had been wonderful, and now she would be coming. We stood or sat or moved about in the silence that was heavy with sorrow and waiting and the knowledge of good-bys that must be said. After a while it was time.

I got up from the chair beside the head of his bed and put my hand on his and said, "Father, I have to go now."

Almost imperceptibly, his head moved up and down— Yes, I know. I stood there, telling him—what?—telling him, "I love you," telling him he was the sweetest father in the world, stooping to kiss him and lay my head against his. His eyes were closed, the veins on his nearly transparent eyelids stood in fine ridges, and tears traced down his cheeks. Through my own tears I could see his face, and I knew—yes, he knows it is good-by, for death, and it is a breaking of the heart for us to say good-by to one another.

But even as I stood there, the tears streaming down my face, I felt a kind of joy for him, a strange gaiety almost, that he would so soon be released, and I had a sense that he stood now on the threshold of some great adventure. He would go, and although he had passed, was passing, through some dark tunnel of sorrow and farewell and the heavy anguish of all of us gathered here—loving him, missing him, suffering it through—he would emerge into a mystery none of us could know. But he would. So it was in a strange way not only a time of terrible sorrow, but a moment of light, as I stood there telling him good-by. I did not speak of it—the light, the strange rush of happiness. I had referred to it once—"I believe we shall know each other again" —that other afternoon, when he had told us he was dying. He had responded with that gesture of—Who knows? I had made my statement then, and it was not the time to blur the purity of this moment by making it again.

And so, in that strange mix of terrible grief and longing and that unexpected surge of joy that came like a gift, like a stranger, I kissed him again, and we left.

In the corridor, holding my arm as we walked along, Stephen said, "He certainly knew what was happening, didn't he?"

"Yes."

In the plane I found my seat by a window, and feeling desolate and composed, I sat looking out onto the field. The other passengers filed in. I turned when a young woman with a small boy paused at the empty seat beside me. "Here's mine," she said, then hurried past and began to settle the child in the single unoccupied seat in the middle of a row three rows back. The child seemed uneasy, and she was trying to calm him.

The thought occurred to me... *Why not?* I stood and went back to her. "If you'd like my seat... you and your son..."

She was inordinately grateful. "Oh, thank you!" She picked up the child and started back down the aisle. The stewardess smiled at me. "That was nice," she said.

I took the seat where the child had been. The two men I sat between were embarrassed and pleased. It was a small thing. But I had done it quickly, with more than customary grace. As I settled in my new place the thought came to me, *Father, I did it for you.*

Waiting....

May 17. I have been home for nearly a week. He is still alive. I've talked with them on the phone—he seems about the same, drifting in and out of consciousness, though some times quite alert. Esther and Roy and the children are there. Esther says it is so helpful to have the children. Mother is still sore from her fall, and her stomach is easily upset. The doctor has given her pills for nausea, but they don't seem to help much.

Our Mary's trip to the doctor turned out well. He took more X rays and examined her again. She doesn't need to wear a brace. It is a wonderful relief. She'll go back for checkups.

I am immersed in my life here, working at finishing my book. I wonder in a way that I'm able to work on it, but I am. The children go to school and are home by early afternoon. Hoyt goes to work and returns. The routines of the day proceed. I think I have never felt closer to Hoyt or felt his support more strongly. I am upheld by it, day and night.

I have gone to a few meetings. One day I went to the noonday midweek service at church. It's a new experiment—an informal gathering of a few interested people. Whoever comes. I've never gone before, but I was in the neighborhood and, on impulse, turned the car down the street toward the church. Hoyt was there, too—the church is only a few blocks from his office—and the two ministers, Bill and Vince. And I. That was all.

Bill had his guitar, and we sang a little, just the four of us. Vince said some things about a passage in the Bible, and we talked about that and prayed. They wanted to know how I was, and my father, and how things were with my family. I told them, and they were loving and compassionate. I felt cared for, and that they would be with me.

My threshold of tears is very low. The slightest thing can set me off—the words of a song, an unexpected noise, some particular evidence of caring on the part of one of the children. I keep thinking of my family in Holyoke. Each time the phone rings I think, *Is this it?*

We've had a meeting here at the house—our intergenerational communications workshop organized through the church to run for six weeks. Hoyt and I and our two teenagers still at home, Steve and Mary, have been attending together. I've missed two of the meetings, because of Chicago and then Holyoke, and I was glad to be back.

We talked about what's going on in our lives now. One of the men has leukemia. It is arrested for the time being, but he wonders—he has been given three to five years to live, and three of those years are up.

I talked about my father. It prompted Debbie, one of the teenagers, to express some leftover grief she had for her grandmother, who'd died two years ago. Then Steve began to sob, in great spasms of grief. He has been so concerned for his grandfather all these months, yet he has expressed little of that. Debbie, who is his friend, went over, put her arms around him, and held him. It was a time of closeness for us all.

May 18. This morning, feeling in despair, I sat at my desk, my head in my hands. I thought, *If there is anything to prayer, let me know it, now.* And what occurred to me was to call Bill and see if I could talk with him. I hated to take his time. I haven't before, but I felt I needed him, and—yes, that I was worthwhile enough—that it was OK for me to ask for his help.

I called the church. I know he's very busy and chances were he wouldn't even be there. But he was and, yes, he'd be glad to see me. I went down, and we talked—about my father, about my mother's future after my father dies, and about how I might fit into that—"I offered, and I'm getting scared. I don't know whether I can...I love her and she needs us."

"There are several of you. You don't need to decide now. She'll need to be in on the decision, too."

We held each other's hands and prayed—for trust, for grace—I don't remember what. It was the talking and listening and understanding and love that healed the part of the despair that would not be dispersed that morning. It was an answer to prayer to think of going there and to go.

Hoyt's birthday. . . .

May 22. We'd wondered, in view of Father's condition, whether we'd be together for this day, but we were. Peter's college term isn't ended yet, but John is home, so there were five of us. We had some of Hoyt's favorite foods—lobster, frozen fruit salad, and a birthday cake decorated, as we always do, with symbols of the birthday person, stick drawings of frosting to represent his new job, some symbols of the music he loves, and of course his family. After we'd finished with the meal and the gifts, I called home to see how things were going.

Roy answered. To my question, "How are you?" he replied, "Not too good."

I said, unthinking, or perhaps still imbued with the birthday mood, "Oh? What's the matter?"

There was a shade of reproof in his voice. "Things are very rough here, Marty."

Of course. How could I have asked such a question? Being this far away it is easy to forget the moment-by-moment anguish that must be theirs. "I'm sorry. I wasn't thinking."

Stephen came to the phone. Esther was at the hospital,

he said. He would be going soon to relieve her. Father's condition seemed very low. There had been several days, since they'd talked with me last, when he'd almost seemed to rally. The doctor had even thought of drawing fluid from his lung again, as though there were reasons for life-expecting measures. But the last day or two he had seemed worse again.

Did they need me? I asked—I'd been home more than a week. I felt caught up on things here and I could come to Holyoke again, if they needed me.

"Well, let's wait a little while," Stephen said. "I'll let you know."

"All right. I'll call in a day or two, if I don't hear from you." How was Mother? I asked. Not feeling very well. She is very sore and stiff and has a lot of nausea; she can't seem to hold anything on her stomach. Esther was OK, and the children were fine—it was wonderful to have them there. We hung up, promising to talk again in a day or two.

Within an hour, Stephen called back. "Martha?"

"Yes, what is it?"

He said, a new urgency in his tone, that Father has seemed very restless, somewhat anxious, all day, but particularly so this evening. "He wants somebody to hold him, all the time. You can't hold him enough." His voice broke with the pain of it.

"Oh—does that seem to help?"

"Yes. It eases him. If you hold him, he relaxes, seems more peaceful. But he has been very uneasy." I felt the pain of it—he who has been so strong, so calm in the face of death. What is he saying? Hold me, comfort me, keep me with you? With the press of your body keep me safe in the face of death? Though I go alone, stay with me? The anguish of it came to me, a thousand miles away.

"So that's what we're going to try to do," Stephen said, his voice calmer now that he had told me. "We're going to try to be with him around the clock, to hold him, if that's what he wants. But we need more people—there aren't enough of us here to cover the hours. Can you come?"

"Of course. I'll come on the morning plane."
We hung up. We would see each other tomorrow. I called the airline and made a reservation. Hoyt will take me to the airport on his way to work.

I felt the need of my family, gathered around. I told Hoyt I would like to ask the children to come and pray with me, with us. Since our children have been grown, our family prayers are usually limited to grace at meals. Their prayer life, or lack of it, is their private business, and I am reluctant to assume... Yet I need them now.

"Why don't you?" he said. So I asked them—John and Steve and Mary—if they would be willing to come into the living room and pray with Dad and me, not because I'm making any assumptions about prayer for them, but because I need them, and it would be helpful to me.

They came immediately, and we stood in a circle on the rug, our arms tight around each others' shoulders, our heads bent so they were almost touching, and we prayed—first Hoyt and then I—acknowledging our grief and our need. We asked of that formless, faceless Presence, which hovers, an intensity of love, that it would be with us, comfort and strengthen us, and give us clarity to be what we need to be, and the assurance of love. Amen. In the shadows at the back of my mind, an image... "Lo, I am with you..."

I thanked the children, then went to the attic and got my suitcase, so recently put away. I packed the nightclothes, the underwear, a bag of cosmetics, some clothes to wear at home and at the hospital. And, yes, choosing it carefully, I laid in the suitcase a dark blue dress to wear for the funeral of my father.

This dear, painful day...

May 23. Stephen met me at the airport, and we drove home. How was Father this morning? He seemed less restless, had been quietly sleeping. They'd not stayed all through the night—Father had gone to sleep and after a while they'd come home. Esther was at the hospital now. Mother was feeling very poor, had not been to see Father at all yesterday. Mary had called from Wisconsin. She would come if we needed her.

We got to the house and went in to see Mother, on the bed in the dining room. Her eyes looked distracted, her face drawn. On the windowsill was some medicine the doctor had given her for the nausea that seems to come whenever she tries to eat. Roy was there, too, doing some paper work at the table. He had fed the children an early lunch, put them to bed for midday naps.

Had we stopped at the hospital? Mother asked. No, we'd come here first. We'd go up there in a few moments. Did I want some lunch? There were things to eat in the refrigerator. No, I'd rather go right away to the hospital.

The air of the house was heavy with what was happening, with the strain of waiting and waiting.

In a few minutes we left for the hospital. At the doorway Stephen turned to me and said, "Now if you think *that's* grim..."

We drove to the hospital and parked the car and, in a wordless dread, went in. We went up in the elevator and through the firedoors, into the corridor from which his room opens. There is a small waiting room—a few chairs and a table with old magazines—in an alcove near his room, and Esther was sitting there, reading a magazine.

"Esther!"

She looked up, her face broke into a smile, and we greeted each other.

"How is Father?" I nodded toward the slightly open door of his room.

"He's sleeping. I was in for a while this morning. The nurses came to bathe him, and after that he seemed restless, and they suggested if I sat out here a little while he might go to sleep."

I nodded, then went toward the door of his room, pushed it open and crossed the threshold. He was asleep, lying on his side, facing me. His upper arm stretched toward the bed rail, and his fingers gripped the rail. His elbow appeared to float in the air. The expression on his face was of a man sleeping. He didn't look particularly different—not more wasted, sicker, than when I'd left ten days ago. I stood and looked at him, watching to be sure his chest still rose and fell. It did—he is alive, my father is alive. I had not come too late.

I thought of going close, to touch him, speak his name, tell him I am here, in case he can hear me, in case it matters and he would like to know—and because I would like to touch him, lay my hand on him. But I did not. I didn't want to disturb his sleep. And I was also fearful—that when he woke he would be restless again, that his condition would demand of me what it would be hard to give, a simple staying there, not shrinking back from his anguish, his difficulty in dying. He might be afraid, and how could I bear that—my father, who has always been strong? Standing in the doorway, I extended my spirit to him, a caress. I stood a moment longer and then, backing slowly out of the room, I drew the door partly closed, as it was before. "He is asleep," I said to Esther and Stephen.

We sat there, the three of us, in a kind of reprieve—that we are together, that we are well and strong, that he has not died yet, that for a few moments we could enjoy our reunion without constant thought of Mother's infirmity or Father's deterioration.

I saw a nurse go into Father's room. She came out again, gathered up from the desk a blood-pressure gauge, and reentered the room. She came out again and drew the door shut and, walking quickly, went to the desk.

Stephen and Esther had seen her, too, but we did not speak of it. Very soon a young dark-haired man who appeared to be a doctor came hurrying through the firedoors and, along with the first nurse and another nurse who had now appeared, entered Father's room. We waited and wondered, and I began to feel it—the relief, the breaking of the thread, some thunder in the depths of the earth, some strange catapulting into an adulthood in which that barrier to death of a father who is still alive is starting to slip—an avalanche creaking, giving way, a widening seam.

The nurses and doctor came out. They did not look at us though they must have felt our eyes on them. The doctor went behind the desk and through another doorway into a back room. As though in a flow of motion not to be broken into, the nurse came over to where we sat; we looked up and she said, her voice even, quiet, "The doctor would like to talk with you because Mr. Whitmore has expired."

"Oh, has he?" We were on our feet, our hands reaching to each other. I felt the wire breaking—a snap of relief—and then I felt a wave of regret, that I hadn't gone to him when I stood in the doorway of his room, that I hadn't stood close, spoken his name—"Father!"—one more time. *I could have. Why didn't I? Partly, because I was afraid. If only...*

We followed the nurse into a small back office, where the doctor sat at a table, signing a paper. I suppose it was a death certificate. He said something about not being very familiar with the case. He thought death came at about 12:20.

He referred to the card from the eye bank—it has been with Father's things—and wondered whether we wanted to go ahead with that donation. Yes. We would have to get our mother's signature on this paper—he gave it to us.

The nurse stood with us in the room. "Can I see him?" I asked, not knowing why I needed to, but I did.

"Yes. It will be hard, but you can. Just a few moments." She left us, and we waited while the doctor finished his paperwork. Then we went out into the hall, and in a moment or two the nurse came to us and said, "You can see him now."

I looked at the others, questioning—Shall I go by myself? Stephen said, "I'll go with you." Esther, who had been with him long hours this morning, said, "I think I'll stay here." She was crying.

Stephen and I went into the room. Our father's body lay there, bent on its side, his face pale and gray, the eyes closed. I looked at his thin limbs, thin as sticks... he is a bird, a frail bird. He is a collection of dry twigs, a puppet figure lying with the string gone slack... Stephen put his arms around my shoulder. "He looks very lifeless, doesn't he?"

"Yes." It occurred to me to reach out and touch him—the body of my father—but I did not. What I needed to do I was doing—standing close to the presence of his death, his body so still now in the mystery.

When did the last life leave him? How was it? A final flicker of energy in the heart? A nerve impulse faltering, then stopping, midway on its journey? Some image flitting in the brain—a flash of a bird in the branches of a tree? How does life go? Do the extremities dull out first?

I do not know. But if we stand close, the truth will come to us—a few moments ago he was alive, and then the balance rod straightened and quivered and tipped, and he is dead. It was over.

In unspoken mutual assent Stephen and I turned to leave the room. The nurse, who had been standing behind us at the door, followed us out. Esther stood there in her bright coat and, her voice breaking, said to Stephen, "Did he look very different?"

"No," he said.

The nurse came to us. There were tears in her eyes. "We all feel bad, too," she said—she for whom the occurrence of death is a common thing.

"Thank you," we replied.

We stayed a few minutes longer, talking with the nurse about what undertaker to call, about the disposition of Father's things. We thanked her and all of them for the weeks of compassionate care. Then together in a wordless closeness, we went through the doors for the last time, down in the elevator, through the lobby that is large and empty, its carpet stretching across an empty floor, out into the sunshine, and home.

We got out of the car and waited to go into the house together. Who was going to tell Mother? We did not say. We entered the house and went toward the dining room, where she was resting on the bed.

She started to sit up when she saw us. "Well, how is he?"—alarm in her voice. I was standing closest. "He's gone, honey," I said.

"He *is*?" She sat upright now, and I stooped over and put my arms around her. "Yes."

"Oh," she said. "Just now?"

"The doctor thought it happened about 12:20."

Still, she did not cry. An anguish too terrible for tears sat on her face. We told her how it was—he'd been asleep, the nurses went in and out, the doctor was summoned. She listened, but I wondered if she was hearing us.... Was she, perhaps, with him? Not now, or yesterday. When? Last week, or last year, before he got sick, or in some haze of comings and goings and being together, decade after decade, from youth to age? Finally she spoke. "He was my *husband*," she said, "for fifty years." There was a note of insistence in her voice.... Was it disbelief that it is over, or that it ever happened at all, or that life can come to this moment of a May noonday when that which was most central to her life is gone, utterly gone? Who can believe it—any of it—life, or death, or sunshine, or grown children standing about, or the coverlet on the bed from which she had raised herself up to learn that he has died? Who can believe it, when the taproot of life is cut through?

Roy was upstairs, getting the children up from their naps. He brought them down. Esther had told him what has happened. He set Craig down on the floor and began to tie the boy's shoes. Esther went over to Craig and, kneeling on the floor beside him, said, "You know I told you Grampa was very sick?" He nodded. "Well, Grampa died today." The child looked startled. "He *did*?" he said.

The house was suddenly alive with activity. There were people to call, arrangements to make. "I'd like to have cremation," Mother said. She has told us before, "After my mother died—nobody had cremation then—I used to have nightmares..."

We agreed we'd have a closed casket at the calling hours and the funeral, then cremation, and burial of the ashes in the family plot. Stephen and Roy left for the funeral director's. They would choose a casket and arrange for times.

We decided to wait before calling Mary. She'd be at work now, but if we waited an hour she'd be home and that seemed a better place for her to receive the news. Esther called Auntie Kate. She is Father's only sister. She was grief-stricken. Esther reported to us, after the call, that Auntie Kate seemed not to have believed Father was that sick.

Stephen called from the undertaker's. Would the funeral on Friday afternoon be all right? He was still trying to reach Mr. Appleton, the minister. We conferred about calling hours. Mr. Day, the funeral director, suggested Thursday afternoon and evening and Friday morning. Esther thinks that is too much for Mother. How about Thursday evening and Friday morning only? That's better.

The weekend coming is a holiday weekend—Memorial Day. The cremation will have to wait until Tuesday morning. We could have the graveside service on Tuesday afternoon. Would that be all right? Yes. We'll all need to stay on for several extra days, but it will be good to have the time together.

There are a few details for the notice in the paper. Mr. Day will send it in. Father had already made obituary notations for himself—his "compendium," he called it. Mr. Day has that. What about flowers? No, we don't want a large array of flowers, though we'll provide a spray from the family. To what charity should memorial contributions be sent? The church? No, they've just received nearly a million dollar endowment. Amherst College? Stephen assures us that the college is rich enough. The Holyoke Hospital maybe? Father has served on its board of directors, and certainly the family has had many occasions of utilizing its services. Yes, we would like memorial gifts to go to

Holyoke Hospital. We finished conferring over the phone. Stephen and Roy will be home soon.

I called Hoyt at work. He will come on the morning plane—the same one I came on this morning. It seems a world ago. He'll talk with each of the children—he'll call Peter, who is probably in final exams. John is home from college for the summer. Steve and Mary are in their last weeks of high school. Whatever they decide will be fine. Hoyt will call back to let me know.

Stephen and Roy returned. They'd chosen a simple wooden casket—"I saw it in the corner, and it looked right for Father," Roy said. Stephen called his wife in Oklahoma. He came away from the phone, tears in his eyes again. "She's very upset," he said. "She loved Father very much."

There were friends to call. Mother wanted to inform the family doctor. He was not at his office. She left the message. We called Mrs. Cox, the friend who has helped care for both Mother and Father in previous illnesses. She wondered what she can do to help. Esther asked if she would stay with the children during the funeral. Yes, and she'd stay on at the house to help us with the buffet gathering for the family and friends from out of town. We called Uncle Harold. He'll come. He sent his love. He'll rent a car at the airport—no need to come for him.

As soon as we thought she'd be home, we called Mary and told her. She has been expecting it. She'll come on the afternoon plane tomorrow. Bruce is in the midst of his exam period and cannot come. He sent his love. We called Cousin Phil's widow in Sunderland. She'll tell her children, scattered over the North East. She was sure some of them will want to come.

We are revitalized with all the activity, and underneath it all, despite the inescapable sadness, is the rejoicing for the marvelous man that he was, the full life he had, and the end of his long ordeal.

The afternoon went on. Phone calls started to come. We drank tea and planned for supper and occupied ourselves with the two little children, who wanted to go outside and play and needed rubbers because the ground is muddy.

In the evening Hoyt called. He relayed the condolences of the men and women in his office. He told me of a man I know slightly—a brilliant man, with a folksy style garnered from years of working with the people of rural Appalachia. He had come to Hoyt to express his sympathy. "When I told him Father was eighty—you'd have to know Tex to understand this—he said, 'Praise the Lord.'" Tears came to my eyes. I understood.

Hoyt had talked with the children. They won't be coming. Three are in final school exams, and John doesn't want to be the only one. In a way I'm relieved. I'll miss them, and they'll be missing something important, too. But I'd feel responsible for them in all this flurry and grief and family recollecting—that I should be an attending parent for them. I can be freer now to savor this experience as one of Father's children, close with the other receivers of his fatherhood, and with Mother—companions in a common history of summers and winters and Christmas afternoons, of eating cheese and oysters and crackers at one gulp, of mayflowers in the woods in early spring, of Red Sox games on the radio on Saturday afternoon, of the aura of Amherst College and the legacy from the army uniform in the trunk in the attic... "In Flanders fields the poppies blow / Between the crosses, row on row, / That mark our place...," of his backyard gardens you couldn't even see from the street.

It is ours—all of it, and this is the time to mark it all, to let it return in its fullness and its terrible transitoriness... And yet, there is a way in which it is part of us all, forever... "Father, you are the blessing."

The day after....

May 24. It is the day between the day of his death and the day of his funeral. We have gone to the airport to get Hoyt, who arrived carrying under his arm a copy of Hurlbut's *Story of the Bible*. It was the version in which his childhood was nourished, and he told me, somewhat abashedly, since neither of us is particularly sympathetic with the custom of carrying a Bible around to proclaim one's identity, that for a long time he's wanted to look it over again and this seemed like a good occasion.

Two hours later we went back again to get Mary. She wants to know how it all was. In a way she minds that she wasn't here with the rest of us when death came.

We've had a visit from Mr. Appleton, the minister, to discuss the details of the service. We've perused the newspaper article—accompanied by Father's picture—on the front page: "Noted Local Attorney Dies." We're pleased to have before us in all those column inches such a listing of his accomplishments and associations—the acknowledgment that he grew up here in Holyoke and was a Phi Beta Kappa at Amherst, a record of his World War I experience, the names of the two law firms of which he was successively a member, his memberships in professional and community organizations, the institutions on whose boards of directors he had served, his religious affiliation. And then his survivors—his wife, his children (yes, our names are spelled correctly), his sister and brothers, "and fifteen grandchildren." Finally, information about his funeral.

The photograph of him is an old one. Stephen had brought a more recent one to the paper, but they'd evidently preferred this. He's not looked like that for fifteen years. But it's a nice picture. It's all right.

And we have talked. Esther recalled a conversation she had not long before Father died, with the foreign-born doctor who had cared for him at the Soldiers' Hospital. "He kept asking me," she said, "'How did he raise you?'" He wanted to know—Was our father strict? lenient? "I have met all his children," he said. "I have small children. I would like to have them be like you. How did he raise you?" he asked again. We are flattered and proud, for Father as well as for ourselves.

At some time during the day, in a kind of surprised declaration, Mother said, "I am a widow," naming her new status. Another time, looking off into some mix of memory and delight, she said to Stephen, with whom she'd been talking, "He loved me very much."

I remember the time when as a small child I got up in the morning and, standing on the rug outside my parents' door, heard my father moaning. Fearing that he was terribly ill, I opened the door and said, to the agitation of bodies under the blanket on my mother's bed, "Is Daddy sick?" I had an immediate sense of jarred perception—this is not what I thought—and after a moment of awkward silence I heard my mother say, "Daddy's just telling me how much he loves me." I left the room, feeling a bit sheepish and puzzled, but not frightened. When later that morning my mother suggested to me very gently that I not come in their room unless I knocked first, I thought to myself, *I won't—you can be sure of that.* It was a world far from my world.

There was very little talk about sex in our growing up. My parents conscientiously read to us the classic children's sex education book, Karl de Schweinitz's *Growing Up*. My mother informed us in plenty of time about menstruation and the event it anticipated—pregnancy and childbirth. But the sexual act itself I did not fully understand until my later childhood—incredible as that seems, now that preschool picture books detail the whole process. But I knew my parents loved each other in some bonding physical way that was different from any exchanges of affection in which I was involved. When the information did come, after I suppose an inevitable psychic jolt that *that* was what men and women did with each other, I found it quite compatible with my knowledge of my parents, a further confirmation of what I knew—that, despite their differences and occasional irritations with each other, they nourished each other in all ways. I rejoice now in my mother's happy quietude when she says, the day after my father's death, "He loved me very much."

Tonight we had our first session of "calling hours" at the funeral home. We'd agreed we wanted the casket closed while we were receiving friends. The funeral director, Mr. Day, wondered whether we'd like an initial viewing for the family. Mother decided that yes, she would. So, well before the seven o'clock start of the calling hours, we drove to the funeral parlor and helped Mother, still limping and sore from her fall, into the building.

Mr. Day was there to greet us. He is elderly himself, an old family friend. He has had a tracheotomy and speaks in the artificial tones of the device in his throat. His face is kind. He led us into the room reserved for our use.

There it was—the coffin, the upper half of the lid raised to reveal the body of a man in a blue suit, a white shirt, a tie with a fine diagonal stripe. Yes, the face looked like the face of my father, though the mouth was not set just right. His glasses sat on his nose, over the closed eyelids. We saw fine marks around the eyes—traces perhaps of the removal of the corneas for transplant. It was all right. The whole thing was all right. I felt strangely removed from the body resting on the satin quilting in a shiny wooden box that in a few days will be consumed by fire. I had seen my father before in his death—that slight figure, bent sidewards, the thin arms crossed at the wrists—the figure of a bird. It has an authenticity this doesn't, filled as it is with contrivance and disguise. I do not mind this. It is another episode, and it is all right.

After several minutes, Mr. Day came forward. "Ready?" he asked. Mother said, "Yes." I looked away, but then looked back as he folded the quilting up over the arms, laid a tissue over the face, and slowly lowered the lid. I had a terrible dragging feeling, deep inside. Hoyt stood beside me, his arm around my shoulder.

The calling hours began. The people came—old friends we hadn't seen for years—neighbors from the summer cottage Father's family had at Laurel Park, friends from church, women who have been his secretary at one time or another throughout his long career, merchants and clerks from stores where he's been known, fellow lawyers, businessmen from the city, neighbors we've seen in their gardening and housework clothes, now dressed up to come and pay their last respects to a man they loved and honored and who lived on the street longer than any of them. They expressed their sympathy to us, they reminisced about old times, we caught up on each other's families. It was not really a sad time—there were laughter and gladness and a deep joy. I recalled the words of Hoyt's father, calling yesterday to express to Mother and the rest of us his sympathy and love, "My goodness, what a man he was!" And again the words of Hoyt's colleague, his erudition tempered by his years among mountain people, "How old was your father-in-law?" "Eighty." "Praise the Lord!"

We keep watch on Mother. She isn't strong anyway and is weakened by her recent fall and affected by all the long months of strain. Once again, she surprises us, managing so well. She sat in the chair, her cane at her side, conversing with the people who come. She remembered names and faces we had forgotten and recalled old associations. "Yes"—to a man who had served with him on the board of directors—"he enjoyed his association with Amalgamated Paper Company very much." Only occasionally, I heard her say to someone, a stridency in her voice, "He wasn't ready to die. He wanted to *live*." It seemed impolite, almost obscene, for her to thrust that up at us, because he *is* dead, isn't he? Our job is to accept that. Besides, in his last weeks, he *did* want to die, to get it over with, since he knew he couldn't be well. Hoyt said, when we talked about it, "What she means is that she wasn't ready to have him die." That helps. But I admire her courage, too, insisting that death is an outrage and an affront. I think of the poem of Dylan Thomas, "Do not go gentle into that good night, . . . Rage, rage against the dying of the light." In a way she is right—he *would* like to have lived, if he could have been well. I remember on one of my early visits to the hospital he reported having read in the paper that if you live to be eighty you have a good chance of living six more years. "Yes, I read it, too," I said, and for a while we were hopeful together.

Soon after nine, we came home. Tomorrow is the day of the funeral.

May 25. We went to the morning calling hours. On our way into the building a widower, an old friend, came up to me and said, "I just want to tell you how fine I think you children have been in standing with your father and mother through all this." He went on to say he knew it had been a long strain, and he'd noted our frequent visits. I thanked him—it means a lot, and he is right. We have done well, all of us, in getting back here several times each to be with them. It has been our need as well.

Inside, another group of friends waited. Dr. Calhoun, the family's doctor, was there with his wife. He stayed for quite a while, chatting with us all. In some ways he seemed a shy and vulnerable man, wanting to share the time with us, but a little uneasy, too. Does he consider it a threat to his competence that Father has died? He seemed genuinely grateful, almost surprised, when we thanked him for his care and concern. After a while he said, "Well, I guess I'd better go and tend the sick." His wife stayed on.

When the time for receiving visitors was almost over, Uncle Harold appeared in the doorway—he had driven up from the airport and come here. He stood, a tall figure, a kind of luminosity in his eyes, smiling his smile of special recognition when he saw us, stretching out his arms to greet us. He went to Mother, went the rounds of all of us, Father's children, and of the friends he knows. He is composed, calm, a special security for us all, because he and Father have been so close, and we know how he loves us, too. We asked about Margaret, his wife. She's had back surgery. She's doing well, he said. She sends her love.

After a while the other visitors left—it was past noon, and time for us to go home for a little lunch and respite before the funeral. Before we went, Mother said, "Harold, would you like me to ask Mr. Day to open the casket, so you could see George?" He thought for a moment, then shook his head, "Yes, I would, if that's all right." Mr. Day was close at hand, and Mother asked him, "Would you open the casket for Mr. Whitmore's brother?"

"Surely." He stepped forward, lifted the lid, removed the

tissue from the face—it has not changed, the mortician's work is holding. Uncle Harold watched, and I heard a sharp intake of breath, and he said, "OK." Mr. Day closed the casket again, and Uncle Harold strode to the row of chairs against the wall and sat down. I went to sit beside him, and he reached out his hand and squeezed mine. "He was quite a fellow—I just wanted to say good-by," he said. There were tears in his eyes.

In a few moments we gathered our things and came home. Mrs. Cox was here, caring for Esther and Roy's children. She had food ready for us, and we ate our lunch. While we were at the funeral, she'd get the table set up for the buffet gathering.

A cousin who had asked what she could do to help, and to whom we'd suggested she might send over a salad, arrived with three platters of food—her husband and son helped carry them into the house.

More cards and notes came in the mail. We gathered around while Mother opened them. She came to one written on three small sheets of tablet paper. She started to read it aloud. Her voice broke, and she passed the note to me—"I can't read it."

I took it from her and began again: "Dear Mrs. Whitmore and family, It was with a profound feeling of sadness and loss, that I started and ended my day on the 3rd floor at Holyoke Soldiers' Home, today." I looked up, then resumed reading. "I am a senior practical nurse at Holyoke Trade High School. On Monday May 14 I started the geriatric section of my training at the soldiers' home. Mr. Whitmore was my assigned patient. I was to have the pleasure of caring for him in his final week at the hospital. I have worked in a hospital 16 years, and have never had the pleasure of meeting a person of such great courage. He always managed a smile and a kind word"—my voice faltered, I was reading through tears—"never offering a complaint. I shall always remember this great man"—my voice broke. I passed the note to Esther, beside me—"I can't read it, either." She continued, "I shall always remember this great man, who gave me a feeling of joy, just to know him and be able to make his last days a little bit more comfortable. I am sure that your loss is a very deep one. I pray that our dear Lord has made him free from all pain, and will give him the happiness and peace he sincerely deserves. May he also bring you all the encouragement and strength you will need in the future. Sincerely, Mrs. Anne Moore."

Esther laid the note down. We were speechless, stunned by this gift, grateful for the acknowledgment of Father and that, in the extremity of the illness that within a week would see him dead, he could make friends with a stranger, enrich her life, bring her so shining an example of courage and goodness that at his death she should be moved to write such a note.

It was time to go to the funeral. With the message of the note still covering us we got in the cars and drove to the funeral home. We went in a side door and into a special section of seats reserved for the family. There were people there already—Cousin Martha from Sunderland—she walks with crutches because of a hip weakness and her crutches leaned against the wall. Two of her children had come up from Boston. Gwen and Joe were there—they had brought us the platters of food. Uncle Harold, Auntie Kate, and Uncle Andy. We greeted them and took our places.

I sat between Hoyt and Mother. I looked toward the other part of the chapel—most of it obscured from our view by the partition set there to protect the privacy of the family. I saw one of Father's former secretaries. She was with him for several years before her marriage. Since her children have grown she's come back to do occasional special work. She'd been to see him in the hospital several times. She was sitting now between two women I didn't recognize. She saw me and nodded and smiled. There were tears in her eyes.

Mr. Appleton took his place behind the casket with its spray of flowers. He was standing up high. I wondered what he was standing on. His white hair caught the light.

The service began.

It was short. Much of it runs together in my mind—as though particular words did not matter, as though what was being noted, paid homage to, was a stream of life which words can only hint at, can echo in their cadence. The minister read the words we had chosen from Tennyson—

> But such a tide as moving seems asleep,
> Too full for sound and foam,
> When that which drew from out the boundless deep
> Turns again home.

He read some words from "Thanatopsis"—"So live, that when thy summons comes...." They are old-fashioned words, of Father's generation, Mother's choice. Good words now.

He read from the Bible. "The LORD is my shepherd, I shall not want...," "Let not your hearts be troubled, neither let them be afraid."

He talked about Father, that he had not known him long, but what a fine man he perceived him to be. He spoke with dignity and a kind of joyous reserve. Father would have liked that.

We prayed together, and the service was over.

People got up to leave. Some of them came to us, to express their love and sympathy. Francine, our neighbor-nurse friend, said, half-indignantly, half-lightly because she does not want us to be disappointed with what has been done, "I could have given a better eulogy for George myself!" What was done is fine—simple, dignified. Father would have liked it.

We gathered ourselves together and came home, and the friends and relatives poured into the house. Mrs. Cox had everything ready. For a couple of hours we ate together and caught up on the news of relatives, and we remembered glad times and talked about Father. Someone said, "Isn't this a nice party? Wouldn't Father enjoy this party!" We all agreed. Someone else said, "Maybe he is." There is a way, certainly, in which his presence was there, circling among us, enjoying the levity, the love, the being together.

Gradually, people said their good-bys and drifted away. Uncle Harold stayed on a while—he'll spend the night with Auntie Kate and Uncle Andy and leave early in the morning. He talked with Mother, about the lawyer handling the will, about considering a trust fund to take care of her business affairs so she'll have only her personal expenses to be concerned about. He reassured her there is money enough to care for her—she doesn't need to worry. If she wants advice from him, he'll be glad to help—he is not, after all, that far away.

He talked with her, and with us, about what she may want to do later, when she'll have had time to consider alternatives for herself. Stay on in the house? Find smaller quarters in Holyoke? Perhaps even consider entering a retirement home—there is one where she has several friends already in residence. Go to live with one of us? The anxiety raised itself in my mind again—What will she choose? How will we handle it, all of us? What about me? It is a question to defer, for now.

We noted how tender and caring Uncle Harold is with her, his brother's widow. He hasn't told us, but Auntie Kate has, that on one of his trips to see Father, Uncle Harold had talked with him about dying—that in his long years in the tuberculosis hospital he had seen many people die, and it was usually no big thing—a quiet slipping away in sleep—and not to be feared. Auntie Kate said Harold had felt the conversation eased Father, brave though he was. I thought of that as I watched Uncle Harold sitting in the chair by Mother's couch and talking quietly with her.

Then he, too, left. We gathered up a little more food to make our suppers, and we rested back on the day. We have gone through hard and good times. We have survived. We are here.

The days between....

May 28. The days between the funeral on Friday and the interment on Tuesday have their own content. I've been writing notes for Mother—thanking people who've sent flowers or memorial gifts, telling people we've not called of Father's death.

There are errands to do. Mary is making copies of Father's will. There are arrangements to be made about the cemetery lot—just where the ashes will go. People call, drop in to see us.

One day Mother was reading the evening paper and called out, "Oh! There's a piece in the Oracle about Father!"

The Oracle is part of the paper's editorial page—a collection of brief editorials, perhaps a poem or other piece by the local citizenry. We rushed to where she was, and she read aloud:

> Holyoke has many good citizens, and George D. Whitmore, who died this week at the age of 80, stood high on that list. A quiet and modest gentleman, he concerned himself with his community...

Mother interrupted the reading to declare, "Mr. Dwight did this." Mr. Dwight is the paper's editor-in-chief, and he and Father have been friends for a long time. She read on:

> You'd have to talk with him a bit before you realized he was a man of unusual intellectual power. He was a student of the law, a careful practitioner who dotted every "i" and crossed every "t." No detail was too insignificant for his careful attention. His colleagues in the Massachusetts bar trusted and respected him. He never indulged in any public fanfare and shunned the limelight. But we always knew where George Whitmore was and that he was ever available for service. He spent all his life with us in Holyoke and earned the genuine respect his fellow citizens had for him.

We were delighted and touched. We looked over her shoulder and read it again to ourselves. Yes, it is a good characterization of him. How he would have been pleased with this statement, printed below a poem written by a fourth grade student to commemorate Memorial Day. Memorial Day... it is a long time since he has donned his khaki uniform and gone to talk at the junior high school, or since I have stood in the hot brick courtyard of Kirtland School, thinking of him as I delivered my Memorial Day recitation: "In Flanders fields the poppies blow...."

I read the article a third time. Yes, it is like him. It tells him well. I offered to write Mr. Dwight and thank him.

On Sunday we went to church—our father's children, home for his funeral—looking for security and faith, making some witness to courage and family solidarity.

Sitting in the family pew—on the right aisle, halfway down—I thought of the hours I've sat here with my parents. When I was young I used to amuse myself by taking my mother's hand, holding her ring finger in the light from the stained-glass window, and watching the rainbows her diamond made on the buff-colored wall. Before my grandfather died, when I was eleven, I eased myself through the interminable pastoral prayers by seeing how many times I could read the church bulletin before the final Amen. After he died, I reformed my ways—I needed the prayers then.

I was baptized in this church, walked across its platform in innumerable pageants and children's day services and youth Sundays. I was married here, going down the center aisle on my father's arm. It is not a modern custom. Brides are not "given away"—belonging to themselves as, in our culture, they always have. But it was the custom then. My father did opt for equality of parenting when on being asked, "Who giveth this woman to be married to this man?" he answered—we had not discussed it though it was the avant-garde response of its day—"Her mother and I do," then stepped back to sit with her, there in her beige lace dress and her pretty hat.

The cluster of parishioners around our pew has changed over the years. The three children who sat in front of us, beside a mother with marcelled waves in her short black hair, have also grown up. One of the two girls has moved away. The daughter with the enviable long sausage curls has daughters of her own and is president of the Women's

League. The son is a member of the board of deacons and helps distribute communion the first Sunday of each month. I suppose they had adolescent turmoils and may have drifted from the church. But they are back now.

I recall others—the lady with the silver hair and silvery voice whose husband left her for a young woman. I remember my parents discussing the husband's defection—the couple were their longtime friends—with irate astonishment. The couple several rows down whose daughter, a girl in my Sunday school class whom I sometimes envied because she lived in a fancier part of town, died of leukemia. The woman my mother took care to befriend, a woman other people viewed as "odd," and who, I learned much later, had an advancing case of syphilis. The elderly spinster who sat in the pew beside ours, and who, on a memorable Thanksgiving Sunday, sent our family into suppressed merriment (it was church, after all) when, after the concluding words of the Thanksgiving Proclamation, "God Save the Commonwealth of Massachusetts"—she responded with a loud mutter, "You can say that again!"

I have come back here often over the years since I left. Today was a fresh leaving, and a fresh return...I see my father opening the hymnal, sometimes lifting his neck to ease a chafing collar, laying his partitioned offering envelope in the plate, resting his squared fingers on the creased trousers of his blue serge suit. He is consulting his list. After the service he will hurry off to talk with several people with whom he has church business.

It is ineffable, mysterious—the juxtaposition of memory against the present, of finite human beings against the great unknown—which we search for, invite, encounter, fear, and, perhaps, come to trust. I am grateful for my father and for my family's presence in this place. I have friends for whom church associations are fearful and punitive, who have won their freedom from that with pain and struggle. I can only begin to imagine the realignment of life that must require. Of course I have reshaped aspects of my faith many times, and will continue to. But somewhere, deep in the substructure of who I have become, is a trust that when we grope into the dark there is something there, some one, to receive us. Grieved as I am at the death of my father, I am grateful for that confidence now.

One afternoon Stephen and I were in the attic, sitting on the floor and going over some old things—he, the last of his college books and papers, and I, some of Mother's and Father's things—to see what was there, against the day when we'd have to decide what to do with it all.

We started talking about Father, our awareness heightened, I suppose, by the sense of old things an attic always holds and by the dimness of the light and the slant of raw wood in the roof beams above our head. We cried and talked, and at one point my brother said, "I think I remember him most vividly at the beach, at Misquamicut, going with him to get fried clams." I thought back to it—how at the end of the season we'd often take a few extra vacation days and drive down to the beaches that he loved—"going back to the salt water" was how he put it, as though that saline medium from which we all came, over time, still had its special pull for him. We'd rent a small cottage a mile or two from the beach and every morning take our suntan lotion, towels, books, magazines, and some makings for lunch and go to the beach. We'd rent an umbrella or two to nest under and stay all day, playing in the surf and sand until we were logy with the water and sea air. Then we'd return to our cabin to shower and change, go out and eat seafood in some restaurant where the sea breeze blew curtains in at the windows, wander a while past the tourist shops—advertising in gold letters on glass windows "Shops in Paris, Watch Hill, Miami" —and go back to our cabin to read magazines until we fell asleep.

The Connecticut beaches were closer, but they were protected by Long Island, and it was the surf that my father loved. So did we, except my mother, who from time to time would plaintively suggest "we could go to Hammonasset," a state park along the Connecticut shoreline where the waters were quieter. We never gave her her fair turn. We should have, but we didn't. Grown up, I went to Hammonasset once and recalled how cavalier we were with my mother's request. But the ocean seemed my father's place, and we went to locations of his choosing. But, whichever beach he chose, we always supplemented our lunch with a few boxes of fried clams bought from oceanside clam bars. My brother's and my father's mission was to search them out and bring them to us.

"I remember his singing old Amherst songs," I said, "shaving in the bathroom in the mornings when we were small." We recalled lines from the songs—"Oh, sometimes I live in the city...," or one in its entirety:

> Get away from that window, my love and my light,
> Get away from that window, don't you hear?
> For there's going to be a fight,
> In the middle of the night,
> And the razors will go flying through the air.

The fantasy of it amused us, back then—it was before the days of gang wars, or at least of our knowledge of them—and I suppose we were intrigued by the contrast between the heady and violent words and our image of our father as a gentle and peaceable man.

We talked about Amherst College, my brother and I, sitting on the attic floor among the books and papers. "They all thought they were somebody special there," he said, referring to his own undergraduate years. "It was very hard to go from that atmosphere to the business of making a living, to not seeing yourself as the best and the rarest, better than other people. It's a strange place."

"It was a special place to Father."

"Yes."

I recalled another time from my early adolescence. I have thought of it these last days since his death. He and I were alone in the living room. I was lying on the couch, and he was sitting in his favorite chair by the fireplace, reading the paper. I wanted to ask him the question, "Do you believe people know each other after death?" I don't know what had set it whirling in my mind, but for several minutes I ached to ask him.

But I was afraid. It would strike his vulnerability, I knew, and mine. He would answer me at too great length, too deliberately, with many qualifications. I would be embarrassed and perhaps cry. I didn't ask. He would have taken the concern too heavily into himself. I do the same thing, though I am trying not to—trying not to internalize the problem, imbue it with my own anxiety, and therefore compound the whole thing.

On another occasion I did ask. It was after World War II, and Father and I were walking home from a meeting at the First Baptist Church, about a mile away. I asked him whether he thought we might have seen the last major war, whether human beings could stop killing each other in these massive ways. It took the whole walk for him to say, with qualifications and diffidences—his own agonizing—that he doubted it.

We came down from the attic after a while, Stephen with his box of books ready to mail home to Oklahoma. The rest of the family were in the kitchen talking, and to Mother's question, "Where have you been?" I said, "Up in the attic, crying, and talking about Father."

Another task Mother has urged on us is to make lists of the choice family possessions and decide among ourselves who is to get what—at such time, whenever it is, that she breaks up the house. It is a difficult job, this further acknowledgment that our childhood is doomed. It is also difficult because several of us want the same things—the cherry table, the antique chest of drawers, the Winthrop desk, the large mirror that hangs in the front hall.

We made our lists, prioritized them, and made ritual threats against one another for wanting what we want. We joked about it, but it is serious business—the memorabilia matters, the *things* matter. The process was long and drawn out, and finally when we had prioritized and collated the lists we sat down for a final bargaining. We proceeded down the lists, in freedom and acquisitiveness and jest and good spirits. Our love and good manners held, and it was done! Esther says she knows of families who have foundered into long-term acrimony, distributing the family goods.

Something else we must do is make provision for someone to stay with Mother. She is still stiff and sore. It will be several weeks before she can be alone. She would like one of us to stay but knows we can't for that long.

We made many calls, rotating among ourselves the task of placing the call, while the others stood anxiously about. We called several community agencies, to no avail. We called women whose names we'd been given who do home care. No one was free to come. We tried a retired nurse we've known for years—no, she's not doing that any more. We were worried. We'll all be leaving soon. Finally Mother, hearing this drama from her bed in the next room, suggested a woman she's known in the church. Her children are grown, and she lives alone—she may even have done this kind of work before.

I placed the call. The woman answered. I started to explain. She didn't let me finish. "Sure, I can come," she said. "We've been friends for years."

"Oh!" I said. The others, getting the message, hugged each other with relief and happiness. On the phone, we talked a minute more about arrangements and the conversation was concluded. I hung up and joined in the relief and gladness. I repeated the conversation to Mother, who was very pleased. "Wasn't that a good idea!" she said.

Late at night, after Mother had gone to bed, we talked about her future. This is fine for now, but what about later? Will she want to stay in Holyoke, where she's lived for more than fifty years—where her friends are, where her church is, where the routines and places and people are known to her? If she does stay, will it be in this house? She can afford it. She has managed very well alone while Father's been ill. The house is a familiar haven. The neighbors are like family.

But they're *not* family. What if she is lonely and needs more care? Will she want to be with one of us?

Esther's children are young and demanding. Her present house has no extra bedroom.

Stephen and his wife are both away all day, teaching. "I don't know whether we...."

I expressed my anxiety about my writing time, the climate of solitude writing requires. "I wish I'd been more cautious, last October. I'd really love to have her for part of each year—six months, perhaps. But all the time, indefinitely..." I didn't say, "until she dies." I cannot bear the thought that I might wish for that, ever, even for a moment. Yet if I felt closed in upon, with no respite...

"We'd be glad to invite her to live with us," Mary said. "I've checked with Bruce." They, too, are away from home much of each day. "But I'm home at lunch, and the children come in and out from school. They'd be extra company and add a lot of interest to her life. And they'd be good help."

"That's very nice of you." I feel a tremendous relief and gratitude at her offer. "Maybe we could divide the time, you and I?" Stephen and Esther are appreciative, too.

We went around and around with it. Stephen's glance swept the room—the fireplace mantel with its row of family pictures, the familiar chairs, the Victorian sofa with the afghan Mother crocheted years ago, the desk, the bookcases with their hundreds of volumes. "In some ways I think she'd be happiest if she could stay here," he said.

We agreed we can't settle it. We'd better go to bed. Tomorrow... We gave each other good-night hugs and went upstairs.

The Interment....

May 29. The day has been sunny and cool. Esther and Roy spent the morning packing up their things. They'll drive home tonight after an early dinner. Mary and Hoyt and I will go early tomorrow morning, and Stephen will leave the following day.

The morning flew by. We had lunch. It was afternoon. The cars from the funeral director would be coming. The neighbor girl came to stay with the children.

Mr. Day, the undertaker, had told us he would bring to the cemetery a bouquet or two of the flowers sent for Father's funeral. Esther suggested we bring some of our own—Father's flowers, things from his gardens. It seemed a lovely idea. I took a jar and went outside and gathered a few boughs of bridal wreath from the front garden. I put them in the jar. Then, off to one side, my eye fell on the patch of wild grasses and weeds—"You need something wild around the place," he said—and I headed over that way. Craig, who had come outside to play, followed me over and, seeing what I was doing, bent to help. He gathered a fistful of daisies, buttercups, long fronds of wild grasses and weeds. We put them in the jar.

Mr. Day's cars arrived. The grownups got in. We waved good-by to the children and drove off, clutching the jar to keep it steady.

The drive to the cemetery took only a few moments. Auntie Kate and Uncle Andy and Mr. Appleton, the minister, had already arrived. We got out and helped Mother over the several yards of grass to the single row of canvas chairs set up to face the family plot, the large gray stone bearing the name "Whitmore." Smaller markers lie around it. Carrie Deming. James Birnie—a Civil War marker beside the small headstone. His son, James Howard, with a marker from the Spanish American War. There are others.

To the right of the large stone was a small mound of earth. On the mound sat a box, about six by eight inches, its exterior looking incongruously like the outside of a styrofoam picnic basket. Mother said, as though to convince herself she had done the right thing, "I believe in cremation." I reached over and squeezed her hand. The slight movement of my body weight caused a shift in the slightly precarious row of chairs. I thought, *That's all we need—to have the chairs fall over.*

Mr. Appleton stood in front of us. He held his service book in his hand. He looked at Mother. "Are you ready?"

"Yes."

He began to read the service of interment. I heard the familiar, beautiful words as comfort, as a ritual of faith which holds in its cadences our longing and our hope. But it was the day, too, that came to me—the clear, bright air, the soft breeze, the wildflowers Craig had picked mixing with the bridal wreath in the glass jar we brought from home. The awareness that the earth on which we were—a bit precariously—balanced, nourishes us, blesses us with myriad delights, and receives the ashes of our bodies back into itself. A gratitude for the sunshine reaching to this tiny patch of earth on the edge of a cemetery where in grief and love a thousand mourners have laid their dead.

We bowed our heads for a closing prayer, and the service was over. We sat a moment in silence. Then we stood and prepared to go home. As we moved toward the cars we noticed two men in workclothes, waiting among the trees. They were waiting to close the grave when we had gone.

We got into the cars and were driven home. The children were running on the lawn.

I stooped to play with Elizabeth. The sun caught her curly hair. With a laugh she turned to run from me, then turned again and, arms outstretched, ran back against my legs, wrapping her arms around them. "I love you!" she said. Tears stung my eyes.

Mother had bought steaks for our last meal together. Roy cooked them on the grill by the back door. We readied the meal and sat down to eat. There was a sense of benediction about it all, and still, a last clinging to what these days have been.

We lingered at the table. Elizabeth was sitting on my lap, daintily lifting portions of food from her plate to her mouth. Her mother admonished her to eat her meat, but she preferred her beans and, against Esther's urging, "Don't eat any more beans, Elizabeth, eat your meat," the child glanced coyly about and picked up a morsel of bean and put it in her mouth. "Your mommy said," I whispered in mock consternation, "Don't eat any more beans." With a laugh, she picked up a bean and ate it. We repeated our little ritual—a joke between us, an illumination.

The meal over, Esther and Roy made their final gathering of belongings. They and the children kissed us all good-by and left. The dispersal has begun. Stephen and I went to pick up the woman who will be staying with Mother. She had been attending a prayer meeting at church. We drove the few blocks to her apartment, where she got her suitcase.

We drove home. She seemed immediately at ease in the house. She suggested that Stephen and Hoyt bring a bed downstairs for her—she'll sleep in another corner of the dining room where Mother sleeps, so she can hear if Mother needs help at night. We are reassured that Mother will be well cared for.

Stephen called his family to tell them when he'll be arriving. He talked first with his wife, then with each of his children. At one point he chuckled, delight on his face. The phone conversation over, he told us, "Daniel said, 'We're going to have Show and Tell tomorrow, and I'm going to tell that you're coming home.'" He's been away for almost three weeks.

All of us, going home....

May 30. In the morning very early Stephen and Mary and Hoyt and I were ready to leave for the airport—Steve to drive us there, Mary to fly to Wisconsin, and Hoyt and I to Tennessee. We awakened Mother to tell her good-by. She was sleepy but said she'd had a restful night. We'd be calling soon.

In the car on the way to the airport Stephen said, "Well, it was done, and it was done right. Now it's time to go back to our lives again." We talked about family reunions—where we can meet for a week or two in the summer—probably not this summer, but maybe next. We acknowledged our closeness with one another and wondered again how only children manage at a time like this. We've been upheld by each other and have been able to offer Mother and Father a support none of us could have offered alone.

At the airport we parted, Stephen to drive back to Holyoke for one more day, Mary to go her way, Hoyt and I to go ours. The flight home was quiet and uneventful—except that I have made this trip several times in the past six months, but this time it was different. It is over—he has died, and the rituals of love and grief have run their course, though there is more to come, I know.

Hoyt had left the car at the airport, and we got in it and drove home. John was there. Mary and Steve were still in school. They'd be home soon. There was a letter from Peter waiting for us. He told of college—the last days of exams and classes and the arrival of the warm days of Pennsylvania spring. He'll be home soon and looks forward to seeing us. Then, at the end, he wrote a sentence that helps to settle the dust, helps me to understand a little more of what has been happening to us all. "I was sorry to hear of Grandpa's death," he wrote, "but I felt a sense of relief for someone who has done a very hard thing."

Home....

June 1. Tonight our, intergenerational group had its final meeting, in our living room. As they came they each expressed their love and sympathy to me. Jim, the man with leukemia, with whom I've felt a special bond, asked quietly, "What was your first thought when your father died?" I said, "I wished I'd gone farther into the room when I first got there, that I'd spoken his name and told him I was there, before he died." He nodded, and it seemed enough—his acceptance of my sense of my own failure, of a final opportunity missed.

Later, as a closing exchange, we were "offering gifts" to one another—one person sitting in the middle of the room, and the others offering words of caring or appreciation. When my turn came I moved into the center. The gifts were generous and warm—wishes for my success in writing, affirmations of my qualities as a person and as a wife and mother. But it was Jim's words that came as a gift beyond measure. "I would wish for you," he said, "the ability to go back in time to that moment in the hospital room, and this time to go in closer, to be with your dad and stand there with him, and to come back out, and to know now that it wouldn't have made any difference." The love and understanding of friends.

June 3. Today was Sunday, and we went to church. I've wanted to say something about Father. Not that they don't know—it's been in the bulletin, and they've called, visited, brought us food. Our house group even sent a contribution to Mother for the memorial fund. So it wasn't to tell them my father had died—it was to place his death in the context of this community of faith and love which has meant so much to us since we moved here a year ago. I wanted to thank them, too, for their love and care, expressed in many ways these past six months—"How is your father?" "Is there anything I can do?" "We love you." And that startling gift of risk and conjecture and faith, "I am praying for you."

I brought with me the piece from the Holyoke paper—the short editorial tribute to my father. When the time came for sharing concerns, I stood up among the rows of wooden chairs set in a wide arc in the remodeled double garage that is the sanctuary of our church and, trying to keep my voice steady, said I wanted to give thanks for the life of George Whitmore, who was my father and who had, as many of them knew, died last week in Holyoke, Massachusetts, at the age of eighty.

A voice called out from the back, "Martha, will you turn around? We want to hear you."
I turned. "I might cry."
"That's all right," she said.
I went on and said a few things about my father and read the piece from the paper and thanked them for their love and care and sat down. Hoyt put his hand on my arm. I was shaking. I heard Bill make some sound of affirmation and felt the healing love of the people flow around me.

It was May 30 when Hoyt and I returned to Nashville—the day after the service of interment in that green and sunlit cemetery. This evening, just four days later, we've had a call from Mary in Wisconsin. She relayed the news, just learned from Mother, that Uncle Harold, who those short days ago had been for us such a presence of stability and love, had died very suddenly at his home in Virginia. He'd gone downstairs to prepare breakfast—his wife still in bed recuperating from her back surgery—and after a while when she'd heard nothing from him, she'd sent her daughter down to see if anything was wrong. He was lying across the couch, dead from a heart attack.

The news burst on me as a mix of sorrow and revelation. As sorrow because we loved him and shall miss him, and we feel for his wife and children in their loss, and because he seemed in full power with a lot of life yet to give and to savor. But it came as revelation, too, of how strong, somehow, are the ties that can bind brothers to one another. When after long months of slowly giving way, one dies, perhaps some resistance to death diminishes in the other, and he dies, too. The diminishment was fed, surely, by the strain and fatigue of Uncle Harold's journey to Father's funeral, but also—it seems to me, stunned by this other death—by some displacement of a part of the heart's home, from here to "there"—wherever, whatever "there" is—so that a child's old game of looking up to, of emulating, an older brother becomes some acquiescence of the will, a lifetime later, to go where he went, to be together again. I know Uncle Harold was deeply in love with life, was looking forward to the wedding of his son, to travel with his wife, to his continuing relationship with their daughters, to work at the agricultural and community projects in which he had invested himself since his retirement. And yet—how does the balance shift from life to death?

In my fantasy—and it is fantasy, all of it, for my faith about life after death includes no defined hunches about scenario and form—I see, through the haze that marks death from life, Father and Uncle Harold in some mutual moment of recognition.

"Bo! I didn't know you were coming"—the glad surprise in my father's voice.

"Neither did I!"—Uncle Harold's slow smile, a chuckle.

"Thanks for coming over."

"Glad to, Bo. I kind of wanted to be with you."

The fantasy stops there, but the good feeling stays and continues to commingle with my feelings of sadness. It comforts me to think—Are the dead lonely?—that these two brothers may be together again.

June 15. I have recently had to get reading glasses—my first since, as an adolescent, I wore those pearly-brown framed glasses for astigmatism. It went away enough after the birth of my first child that for twenty years I've worn no glasses at all. But it was getting hard to read maps, and the names in the telephone directory blurred together. So I got glasses, and things are better now.

But whenever I take them off and return them to their case, I see Father as, in the tendons and muscles of my hand, I mirror his motions as he put his glasses away. I have the same mold of case—maybe that's it—a hard flattened cylinder with a hinged flap that snaps shut. I didn't realize, before I found myself following his motions like a dance of the hands, that I had ever noted how he put away his glasses—folding the earpieces first, laying them against the flattened plush of the case, folding over the flap, snapping it with a graceful deliberation. It must have been when he was settling for sleep. Perhaps I had come in to kiss him good night. It can't have happened often—the years I lived in the house with him were years when he would tuck me in, not vice versa. Yet this motion of mine brings him so sharply to mind, and I see his veined hands, the squared joints flexing, laying his glasses—and his day—so carefully and confidently to rest.

Summer

A month....

June 24. Father, it has been a month now. The fireflies on the lawn are flickering star points tonight, and the mimosa tree is a spreading fern against the gathering dark—the leaves are closed for the night. Mary is sitting on the steps playing her guitar and singing, and the boys and I—Hoyt is away—have just come back from a ride in the country where we stopped suddenly so that Peter could watch a bird and be sure it was an indigo bunting. It was. The southern summer is lush and green, and I wish you were here to see it.

Last summer, when we first moved down here and the heavy greenness of it all came as such a daily surprise, I thought of you often, and how I would show it all to you—how pleased you would be with the way things grow, how you would enjoy watching the birds and chipmunks come close to the window to eat, how you would love the sound of the crickets at night. I wanted to show you the house—our first house after all these years of being married and living in houses that were never our own. I knew the places you would linger—the corner window where the tree stands right outside and beyond that other trees and the lawn and the trees of the neighbors across the street—but hardly their houses at all—just glimpses of houses among trees.

We have a streetlight at the bottom of our lawn, and it comforts me. Tonight the light from it was a small moon, our very own, local, technological moon, but lovely. I thought of all those long summer evenings when the neighborhood children would gather by the streetlight at the edge of our lawn back home and play—Hide and Seek, Statue, Kick the Can—and how I felt part of a gang in a way I never had before, and how we would play into the darkness until, one by one, our mothers called us home.

It all worked together—the fireflies and the mimosa tree and the indigo bunting (how you loved birds, and such identifications as I can make, which are few, I learned from you) and the street lamp—they all turned my thoughts to you, and the longing I have felt sweep over me these past weeks came again. I said to Mary, "It's all so beautiful—and I miss Grandpa." She murmured a sound of acknowledgment and understanding and after a while began to sing again, "All my trials... soon be over." And I remember how you were—sick and frail and steadfastly resolved to be on about the business of dying—and I do not wish you back into that. But if you could come for a little while, as you were a year ago, or two—*that* I would wish for, just for a little while, just for your child who, middle-aged and lonely, longs for your presence again and, for this moment, yields no tender to reason.

That figure of the bird—your body like a frail bird—came back to me. Was it the indigo bunting that brought it back? In the plane on the way home I had made some notes. Tonight after I came inside I got out the notes and began to write a poem that has been shaping itself in my mind. For now, it says what I need to say, to keep you from slipping away. I am not ready to let you go.

Father, frail bird, strength only in the grip of the hand
Holding our hands, holding the bed rail, grasping for a
  stay and waiting for death—
Father, winter-tree, leafless in winter, stark-branched
  and holy,
The eyes illumined yet, the smile faint and fleeting—
  "You have a strong constitution," he says to you, waiting.
  "I thought as much," you say, and smile, waiting for death—
Father, strength of our life, where shall we look for you?
  How shall we go without you? Who will stand at the
  curbside and wave, seeing us off on our journeys—
    to college, to marriage,
    the summer visits over, off on our journeys
    south, west, wherever, back to our life?
Father, in whose eyes the tears shone, who will weep for us
  now?

—M.H.

Epilogue

It has been almost a year now since he died. The months have run full circle, and we are back to May again. My year's writing project has been this—this dealing with the death of my father through these pages of love and grief and memory and joy. It has been a good thing for me, to hold him—and us—in this way for a while. To have lived through it all once in actuality and, through the gift of recall and discernment, to live through it again in a different way. To be a writer is to know the true economy of experience—nothing is wasted, everything is for use, everything is redeemable. Even grief. Even loneliness. Even pettiness and selfishness, and that in us all which, from time to time, puts us in the center of the stage while all the world goes round. I do not excuse it or condemn it. It is there. Rejoice.

The rest of us have "gone back to our lives," as my brother put it. But we have been back, each of us, to the white house where we lived together for all those childhood years and to which we returned, more frequently than usual, during the months of his illness. Mother lives there now with a woman who helps care for her. The agonizing questions of where she might most happily and productively live have come to rest here, at least for now. The neighbors still live in their houses up and down the street.

Last fall I went up to Holyoke to help my mother celebrate her eightieth birthday. We went shopping—not the gala all day affair we used to do once or twice a year, replete with lunch at our favorite tearoom, but a brief trip commensurate with her strength. We bought her a pants suit—her first, now that she is eighty. She was delighted with her adventurousness, and wistful—"Father would like this," she said, fingering the fine brown cloth, the rose-colored sweater we bought to go with it. She stopped at the perfume counter. "I want to buy some perfume, from Father"—her voice catching. "I suppose it's silly."

"It's not silly at all," I said. How does one indulge one's self to compensate for the loss of a lover of fifty years? "It's not silly at all. Anything."

Recently, I went back again to visit her, to see old friends. It is spring now. The afternoon before I left I went around the yard slowly, touching the barks of trees, lingering by the gardens, fixing in my mind once more the way the tree branches spear into the sky above the roof of the garage.

At the back of the house is on old wisteria vine. Mother tells me it hasn't bloomed since they had to have it trimmed the last time the house was painted. I remember when wisteria vines bloomed two floors up, by the sleeping porch, and the fragrance of wisteria drifted past the awnings to spice the air above our beds as we slept. The trunk of the vine is thick now, gnarled and gray. A support post to which it was initially attached has been broken in two by the force of the ascending vine, and the upper part of it now winds upward, mingled with the vine and so gray and gnarled you can scarcely tell the one from the other. It impresses me how that which was put there to encourage a young vine has been taken over and finally broken by the life it supported. And yet it stays—integral, attached, interwoven.

I stood and looked at it for a long time and tried to imagine what it looked like years ago, when the vine was young and the post a straight slab of new wood. I couldn't. It must have been this way for a very long time, but I hadn't noticed it before. I trust the vine will bloom again.

I continued on my pilgrimage, past the garage now emptied of the car that Mother sold the last time the insurance came due. The garage door was locked. I peered in at the windows. In the sunlight that came in through the windowpanes I saw Father's garden tools, dusty, leaning against the walls, and I remembered his foot on the shovel, and the sudden jerk as he dug down into the ground to form the edge of the garden. Behind the garage is the steep bank, covered with trees and dead leaves, going down to the backyards of the neighbors who live on the street below.

I walked up toward the house, along the north side, where moss has replaced the lilies of the valley that were my mother's favorite sign of spring and where the apple tree has spread so wide that in the circle of shade beneath it grass no longer grows. I went in the front door. I would come back again, but for how long and how many times, who could know? My father's presence and his absence permeate this house.

I am in a way loathe to finish this, my work, for then I shall have to relinquish him again. I'm sure it's no accident that, in the absence of deadlines and only my own internal clock to direct the progress of these pages, I am come to the end within two weeks of the anniversary of his death. I have felt an urgency these past weeks that I must finish before then, as though time would run out on me and my intention fail. Yet not too soon, either.

Can I release him now from these pages, acknowledging, still, that we shall meet again? Can I be glad for him, remember him, see him reflected in my mother and my brother and sisters and myself—"You look more like your mother, but you have your father's eyes"—and in the grandchildren in whom he took such delight and who now make his lists, crumple the edges, and leave them lying about, and let him go? I hope so. I have, as I said, done this for myself, to deal with grief as well as with my love for him, with all our loves for him.

I have done it for my father, too, and it was what I wanted to do—put him at the center of the stage for a little while longer so that, before the light fails, his tenure on earth can be extended, his sweetness celebrated once more. "He never indulged in any public fanfare and shunned the limelight," the piece in the paper said of him. "Public fanfare?"—never. But shunning the limelight? I'm not so sure. He liked acclaim as much as any man, but it was not in his nature to do those things that make for acclaim. So, Father, this is for you, a bouquet of flowers handed across the apron of the stage. May cheers ring out, may shouts of "bravo!" fill the air. You will demur, step backward, pass it off with your quiet humor. But your eyes will shine, your arms reach out to receive the bridal wreath, the mayflowers, the daisies, the tall wild grass—and all of us who throng forward to encircle you with love.

Eternal God, who committest to us the swift and solemn trust of life: We thank thee for all fair memories and all living hopes; for the sacred ties that bind us to the unseen world; for the dear and holy dead who compass us as a cloud of witnesses, and make the distant heaven a home to our hearts...

Father, in your mystery, be on about your life, your journey from strength to strength. But hover close, too. Wait for us, dear, you who can be anywhere...

"Oh, sometimes I live in the city, and sometimes I live in the town...." He is singing there by the bathroom sink in the morning....

Look down on us. Love us. We miss you still.

And grant, O Lord, we beseech thee, that we who rejoice in the triumph of thy saints may enter with them into an inheritance incorruptible and undefiled, and that fadeth not away.

AUTHORS GUILD BACKINPRINT.COM EDITIONS are fiction and nonfiction works that were originally brought to the reading public by established United States publishers but have fallen out of print. The economics of traditional publishing methods force tens of thousands of works out of print each year, eventually claiming many, if not most, award-winning and one-time best-selling titles. With improvements in print-on-demand technology, authors and their estates, in cooperation with the Authors Guild, are making some of these works available again to readers in quality paperback editions. Authors Guild Backinprint.com Editions may be found at nearly all online bookstores and are also available from traditional booksellers. For further information or to purchase any Backinprint.com title please visit www.backinprint.com.

Except as noted on their copyright pages, Authors Guild Backinprint.com Editions are presented in their original form. Some authors have chosen to revise or update their works with new information. The Authors Guild is not the editor or publisher of these works and is not responsible for any of the content of these editions.

THE AUTHORS GUILD is the nation's largest society of published book authors. Since 1912 it has been the leading writers' advocate for fair compensation, effective copyright protection, and free expression. Further information is available at www.authorsguild.org.

Please direct inquiries about the Authors Guild and Backinprint.com Editions to the Authors Guild offices in New York City, or e-mail staff@backinprint.com.

Printed in the United States
97698LV00002B/140/A